THE LAWYER M

- What do these guys study for three years in law school?

- What are they saying when they approach the judge during a trial and whisper out of earshot of the jury?

- What are all those documents they always carry around?

- Why are they always talking in Latin?

- Why are they always wearing gray suits?

To find answers to these mysterious legal rituals that would normally require years of study in the school of hard knocks, the book to research is . . .

STILL
THE OFFICIAL
LAWYER'S HANDBOOK

DANIEL R. WHITE, a native of Atlanta, practiced corporate law and litigation for several years in Washington, D.C., before devoting all his time to writing and lecturing. As well as being the author of four best-selling books of legal humor, including *Trials & Tribulations: An Anthology of Appealing Legal Humor* (available in a Plume edition), he is a favorite speaker at bar association gatherings and law schools. He lives in Washington, D.C.

Other Books by Daniel R. White

*Trials & Tribulations: An Anthology
  of Appealing Legal Humor**

*White's Law Dictionary**

*What Lawyers Do . . . And How to Make Them Work for You**

Look Homeward, Angel

King Lear

The Autobiography of Alice B. Toklas

Michelin's Guide to Yugoslavia

The Old Testament

The Joy of Cooking

The Joy of Sex

Gray's Anatomy

*Especially recommended.

STILL
THE OFFICIAL
LAWYER'S
HANDBOOK

DANIEL R. WHITE

A PLUME BOOK

PLUME
Published by the Penguin Group
Penguin Books USA Inc., 375 Hudson Street,
New York, New York 10014, U.S.A.
Penguin Books Ltd, 27 Wrights Lane,
London W8 5TZ, England
Penguin Books Australia Ltd, Ringwood,
Victoria, Australia
Penguin Books Canada Ltd, 10 Alcorn Avenue,
Toronto, Ontario, Canada M4V 3B2
Penguin Books (N.Z.) Ltd, 182–190 Wairau Road,
Auckland 10, New Zealand

Penguin Books Ltd, Registered Offices:
Harmondsworth, Middlesex, England

Published by Plume, an imprint of New American Library,
a division of Penguin Books USA Inc.

First Plume Printing, November, 1991
10 9 8 7 6 5 4 3 2 1

Ⓟ REGISTERED TRADEMARK—MARCA REGISTRADA

LIBRARY OF CONGRESS CATALOGING IN PUBLICATION DATA:
White, D. Robert (Daniel Robert)
    Still the official lawyer's handbook / Daniel R. White.
    p.   cm.
    Rev. ed. of: The official lawyer's handbook. c1983.
    ISBN 0-452-26694-7
    1. Law—United States—Anecdotes. I. White, D. Robert (Daniel
Robert). Official lawyer's handbook. II. Title.
K184.W475 1991
340'.023'73—dc20   91–19304
                                                  CIP

Printed in the United States of America
Set in Garamond Light

This book is dedicated to Dad, my brother Ben,
Aunt Mary, Uncle B.B.,
Uncle John, Granddad,
Great Uncle Pettus, Cousin Pollard,
Cousin Lee, Cousin Steve, Jr.,
Cousin Steve III, Cousin John,
Cousin Amy, and all the
other lawyers in my family.

CONTENTS

Thanks

To Martin J. Yudkowitz, J.D., Columbia, 1979, my friend, classmate, mute court partner, and the most relentlessly plagiarized source of material for this book. Mr. Yudkowitz provided all the truly clever material not only for this book but for countless other books, although Messrs. Mailer, McMurtry, Wolfe, le Carré, and Seuss have yet to acknowledge their debt publicly.

To Michael Goodman, the cartoonist for this book, who already has people referring to Honoré Daumier and James Thurber as the Michael Goodmans of their day.

To John Freund and David Porter for their initiative and creative assistance; to lawyers Paul "A Pole Attachment Is a Beautiful Thing" Glist, Randy "Community Service, Maybe— Jail Time, Never" Turk, and Dave "The Awesome One" Wescoe, who contributed portions of this book; and to Professors Phil Frickey, U. Minnesota, and Leslie Levin, Columbia, for their legal expertise.

To lovely-but-sometimes-amazingly-tough lawyers Elizabeth Merritt and Lisa Robertson, who tried to keep this book politically correct; to lawyers Dan Attridge and Mary Ann Bernard, who offered helpful ideas; and to Hrothgar Turk, who kept the precedents on all fours.

To Drs. Phil Gold, Laurie Massing, Nancy Petersmeyer, and Sibyl Wescoe for their psychological contributions; and to Dr. Dale Adler, my personal physician.

And, finally, to Debbie Knopman, Ginger Mackay-Smith, and lawyers Missy Asbill Attridge, George Covington, Bill Hannaford, Dave Hayes, Liz Hayes, Jamie Kaplan, Paul Pien, Jim Moody, Janet St. Amand, David Wescoe, Chris Wright, and Martin J. Yudkowitz, who allowed their pictures to appear in this book.

INTRODUCTION

Recession, depression, meltdown —however you want to refer to that awfulness that began sometime in the late eighties and continues even as this book goes to print—the verdict is now in: The legal profession has been hit by it, too—as if we were just an ordinary part of the American economy. As if law were a . . . *business.*

Gone are the days when "growth," "expansion," and "Buy that recruit another drink!" were the expressions most frequently heard echoing through the halls of lawyerdom. Today's bywords are "caution," "retrenchment," and "Pass me a barf bag—quick!"

We've all seen the signs of the leaner, meaner nineties— junk-bond purchasers losing their capital, S&L depositors losing their savings, the poor losing their hope. But can any of these compare with the heart-rending sight of a lawyer losing his Persian rug?

Some things are just too painful to contemplate.

Hence the rush of patriotic Americans to donate food, clothing, even the second family car to the nearest suffering lawyer.

To be sure, the hard times haven't hit every sector of lawyerdom equally. Bankruptcy lawyers, for example, have never had it so good. As company upon company swirls down the tubes, carrying banks, S&Ls, and Rhode Island with them, the lawyers who specialize in corporate euthanasia are prospering. They spend long, profitable hours wandering desolate corporate battlefields, firing bullets of mercy into the heads of slowly expiring airlines, real estate trusts, and business associates of Neil Bush.

Dirty work, but hey, *life* is dirty. Ask the guys who have to clean up after those Budweiser Clydesdales.

Still, times are hard for lawyers as a group, starting with law students. Fewer and fewer firms are sending recruiters to law schools these days, because

*"Before he went to law school, he either agreed or disagreed
with my opinions. Now he concurs or dissents."*

clients are broke, which means law firms are broke—and the demand for new associates who know squat about anything useful has plummeted.

It's not as if associates who got in when times were better are enjoying complete security, either. The D.C. office of the country's second largest law firm made one partner out of thirty-one under consideration this past year—*one* out of *thirty-one*! At New York's biggest firm, the usual six-month grace period for associates told to take a hike has been cut to three months—and the word on the street is that it's going down to an hour and a half.

And this past year, average associate compensation in New York did the unthinkable: After decades of regular, sizable increases, it actually declined—only by about two percent, but a little seems like a lot when it comes to the one thing about your job that makes it worthwhile to get out of bed in the morning.

There is no safety now even for partners, traditionally as immune from quality and productivity requirements as federal judges. Senior partners are being eased out or unceremoniously dumped, as if they were . . . associates. And because of what? Mere *dispensability*—which in preceding decades was virtually a badge of honor for a lawyer,

the quintessence of lawyerosity.

Some say the bad times are just temporary, and in any event the only people getting the boot are those whose firms were already looking for an excuse to get rid of them—dead wood. Maybe, but consider the implications: If you weed out the slowest five runners in a ten-person race, the average pace goes up for everyone. Law firms are speeding up, going faster and harder than ever—and it's going to be that way for a long time to come.

A kinder and gentler profession? Hardly.

A thousand points of light? More like a thousand pints of blood.

So what, you ask?

For most people, news about starving lawyers carries its own justification. It's inherently pleasing.

But if you're a lawyer yourself, in the process of becoming one, or even just thinking about it, the "so what" is that the competition in the legal profession is more vicious than ever. You need all the help you can get.

You need this book!

Still the Official Lawyer's Handbook walks you through every step of your legal career, from puberty to partnership. Starting with that make-or-break first year of law school, it provides enough key concepts

TWENTY-ONE GOOD REASONS
TO BECOME A LAWYER
(WHY NOT? EVERYONE ELSE IS.)

1. The money.
2. You overslept on the morning of the business boards.
3. Your college major was English, History, or Political Science—which, along with a valid driver's license, *might* qualify you to drive a cab.
4. Your Uncle Herb is a lawyer.
5. You think people who carry briefcases look important.
6. The money.
7. You're brilliant, you know it, and becoming a lawyer is the best way to make sure everyone else knows it.
8. You want to change the world.
9. You want to own the world.
10. You're Jewish and don't want to be a doctor.
11. You're a WASP, and your parents don't want you to break a seven-generation succession of lawyers going back to your great-great-great-great-grandfather Biff, who came across on the *Mayflower* with his wife Muffy.
12. The money.
13. You think you look good in pinstripes but don't want to join the Mafia.
14. When you were twelve, you spent your entire summer earnings on an electric train that broke down in two hours, and since then your sole purpose in living has been to sue the swine who sold it to you and reduce him to servile, spit-licking beggary.
15. The money.
16. You were a high school or college debater and still love to hear yourself talk.
17. You think most male lawyers look like Victor Sifuentes or Arnie Becker.

18. You think most female lawyers look like Grace Van Owen.
19. You think a law degree would assist you in your long-term goal of becoming a zeppelin mechanic.
20. You want to teach law because it's common knowledge that law professors have lots of casual sex with their students.
21. The money.

and buzzwords to put you at the top of your class—as well as into bed with at least two of your classmates by Christmas break.

This book is more than just a ticket to success in law school, however. It's an *alternative* to law school, offering better preparation for a legal career than anything you could get at Columbia or Stanford. It offers not only obscure jargon and archaic concepts, but sufficient training in the arts of hair splitting and issue obfuscation to enable you to alienate complete strangers in the space of just minutes —a skill that some lawyers don't acquire for weeks.

All this for under nine dollars.

Law schools are understandably hostile to this book: It renders them obsolete. As of this printing, twenty-nine state bar commissions are actively considering this book as a substitute for law school—which would not only advance the le-

gal profession but also save you thousands of dollars and years of your life. (*See* chart on page 7.)

If you're already out of law school, this book is all the more critical. It shows you how to get into one of those prestigious, high-paying, white-shoe* law firms and, more difficult, how to survive once you're there.

You didn't go to law school so you could spend the next five or ten years dealing dope or selling fire alarm systems door-to-door. You've already done those things. You're ready now for the status that comes from doing something truly useless. You're ready now to be a lawyer.

And not just any kind of lawyer. You don't want to spend your legal career chasing am-

---

*No one actually wears white shoes at these firms. White socks are just fine, however.

SEVENTEEN HARD FACTS TO CONSIDER BEFORE GOING TO LAW SCHOOL (DO YOU REALIZE WHAT THOSE GUYS *DO*?)

1. The average lawyer earns less per hour than a bus driver (although they get about the same amount of exercise).
2. The odds are three-to-one that you personally will not do as well as the "average lawyer" (see Hard Fact No. 1).
3. Everyone you know hates lawyers.
4. The thought of spending eighty percent of the rest of your waking life in a climate-controlled office behind a desk makes you want to upchuck.
5. Partners in law firms can be fired, just like anybody else—and are.
6. The latest census establishes that seventy-eight percent of all lawyers are wider at the stomach than the shoulders and resemble pears.
7. People charged with murder and rape—your likely clients, if you go into criminal law—are usually guilty as sin.
8. Thirty-one percent of all lawyers have ulcers bigger than John Candy's hula hoop.
9. The number of law grads who get jobs with established firms is about the same as the number who end up as short-order cooks—and the latter are happier.
10. Saddam Hussein was a nice guy before he went to law school.
11. A "light day" in a large law firm runs from 8 A.M. to 8 P.M. A "light week" in a large law firm consists of six-and-a-half light days.
12. Dan Quayle is a lawyer.
13. The lawyers who spend the most time in court tend to wear lime green leisure suits and carry Naugahyde briefcases.
14. Arnie Becker gets more sex in one episode of *L.A. Law* than five hundred real lawyers get in a year.
15. Most male lawyers look more like Stuart Markowitz or Douglas Brackman than Arnie Becker.
16. So do most female lawyers.
17. Studies show that the average law professor has only 7.3 sexual encounters with law students per year.

"We practice law to make money, Herwitz. If you have a more compelling reason to practice law, let's hear it."

bulances—which is hell on your dress shoes. You don't want your office to consist of the trunk of your car or the phone booth at the Amoco station across from the courthouse.

You want to be a legal honcho—an adviser to senators, bank presidents, and other big-league criminals. You want a plush corner office, embossed stationery, a genuine leather briefcase, and a secretary who'll screen United Way fund-raisers.

This book tells you how.

This book is designed not just for lawyers, however. It is equally for "lay people" (what lawyers call the people they screw).

Who among us has not at one time or another said, "I'll sue the bastard!" The rub is, only a lawyer knows *how* to sue the bastard. If you, a lay person, want to file a lawsuit, you have to hire a lawyer—which, like hiring a prostitute, may be easy but not cheap.

ALTERNATIVE LEGAL EDUCATIONS: *YOU* MAKE THE CHOICE

Rank	Institution	Cost of Degree* (tuition, books and living expenses × 3 years)	Average Starting Salary	Ratio Decidendi (average starting salary/costs)
1	*Still the Official Lawyer's Handbook*	$8.95 (tax deductible)	$60,000	6,703.91
2	Larry's Legal Institute of Duluth	$1,700	$4,900	2.88
3	University of Texas	$21,000	$35,500	1.69
4	Berkeley	$35,500	$36,500	1.02
5	Columbia	$55,000	$51,500	.93
6	Georgetown	$45,000	$39,100	.87
7	Stanford	$55,000	$46,200	.84
8	Harvard	$66,000	$54,100	.82
9	Yale	$65,000	$53,300	.82
10	University of Mississippi	$12,000	$12,000, 11 bags of cotton, 7 head of chicken, 2 possums	cannot be calculated

*Some of these figures were calculated from data provided by the schools indicated. Others were taken from secondary sources publicly available. Most were fabricated out of thin air. None should be relied upon other than to decide what to do with the rest of your life.

The legal profession is too important to remain veiled in secrecy. It pervades our existence. Whether you want to get out of jail, get out of your lease, get out of your marriage, or just get the hell out—you need a lawyer.

But you don't have to be at your lawyer's mercy simply because up to now you've never understood what he was up to. Dealing with lawyers doesn't have to be like dealing with doctors or auto mechanics—who at least give you a scar or a greasy steering wheel to show for your money.

After reading this book, you'll know where your lawyer is coming from, how he got there, and just where "there" is.

You'll know what lawyers do—and how to keep them from doing it to you.

About the Author(s)

This book was a collaborative effort (unless you're really attractive and consider everything in here extremely witty—in which case I wrote it entirely

"Let me get this straight: The perpetrator, a blond Caucasian female, trespassed on your grounds, broke and entered into your dwelling, sat on your chairs, consumed your porridge, and slept in your beds—is that correct?"

by myself and can be reached through my publisher; photo appreciated). Our composite résumé includes seven federal court clerks, three editors-in-chief of law reviews that libraries actually stock, and—what the hell? it's time they got credit—four justices of the U.S. Supreme Court.

The names of these contributors cannot appear here. Those with families or large debts (the former usually include the latter) can't afford to jeopardize their jobs. Also, as good lawyers, they know the importance of never confessing to anything.

So I have to take all the blame.

For my protection, I hereby state that all characters portrayed directly or indirectly in this book are fictional. *(Right.)* Any resemblance to living persons or practicing lawyers is coincidental and for them, presumably, quite embarrassing.

For anyone offended by any portion of this book, let me just say that it was always my intention to irritate you personally.

CHAPTER ONE

DETERMINING YOUR LEGAL QUOTIENT

Is Your Mind a Steel Trap . . . or a Blocked Bowel?

Not everyone is cut out for a legal career. Before commencing the legal equivalency training in this book, take the following self-assessment quiz to determine whether you have the right stuff for the law.

You might discover that you really aren't suited to it at all—better to find out now, before your vocabulary is permanently encrusted with Latin. You might also discover, if your score is too high, that you aren't suited to anything else—in which case this book will prove to have been the best investment of your life. (Answers and a grading scale appear on page 15.)

Legal Quotient Exam

1. When you wake up each day, the first thing you do is:
   a. Hit the snooze control.
   b. Turn on the afternoon news to see what you missed that morning.
   c. Try to ascertain the age, gender, and species of whatever is sleeping beside you—without waking it up.
   d. Make the bed, polish your shoes to a high gloss, write a letter to Mother, and recite five sections of the Internal Revenue Code—all before breakfast.

2. If your boss told you that your next assignment would be to proofread the entire Encyclopaedia Britannica, you would:
   a. Lose your lunch on the spot.
   b. Explain that as flattered as you are to receive so significant an assignment, just yesterday you heard Teitell down the hall saying he dreams of such work, and you'd be willing to stand aside for Teitell in this instance.
   c. Accept the assignment cheerfully—and then call your stockbroker to short as many shares of Encyclopaedia Britannica, Inc., as he can lay his hands on.
   d. Say you don't see any reason why you couldn't complete the job by next Monday.

3. When you were a child, you experienced lust in the presence of:
   a. Your parent of the opposite sex.
   b. Your parent of the same sex.
   c. Either parent's briefcase.
   d. Your Great Dane Gaylord.

4. *Word association.* When you hear the word *prison*, the first thing that comes to your mind is:
   a. Your last income tax return.
   b. Violent criminals.
   c. Unsafe sex.
   d. Establishing an alibi.
   e. All of the above—in that order.

5. When you watch *Perry Mason* reruns, you root for:
   a. Hamilton Burger.
   b. Warren Burger.
   c. Della.
   d. Perry.
   e. Ironside.

Perry Mason—
A Lawyer's Lawyer

6. If a sexual opportunity presented itself right now, you would:
   a. Go for it—no matter where you are, who you're with, or what it might do to the rest of your life.
   b. Ask whether s/he is on some form of birth control, has been to Haiti within the past ten years, or has ever done time in a maximum-security prison.
   c. Call all your friends to let them know it's finally about to happen.
   d. Be too surprised to act.

7. *Word association.* When you hear the word *security*, the first thing that comes to your mind is:
   a. Blanket.
   b. Police lock.
   c. Stocks and bonds.
   d. Malpractice insurance.

8. Your idea of a great time is:
   a. A late night at the office proofreading franchise contracts.
   b. Around-the-clock negotiations on a corporate takeover.
   c. Foreclosing on a widow with six young, learning-disabled, physically handicapped kids.
   d. Nothing remotely resembling any of the above.

9. Your favorite color is:
   a. Caribbean blue.
   b. Conference-table brown.
   c. Green—broken up by pictures of former presidents.
   d. Yellow, preferably 8½" × 14", with narrow margins.

10. When you think of lawyers, you envision people who:
    a. Protect the downtrodden.
    b. Screw the proletariat.
    c. Couldn't get jobs in productive sectors of the economy.
    d. You try not to think about lawyers.

11. Which of the following do you consider most likely to guarantee success in the law?
    a. A precise, analytical mind.
    b. Thirty charcoal gray suits with vests.
    c. The ability to lie like a politician.
    d. This book.

12. When you look at the following ink blot, the first thing that comes to mind is:

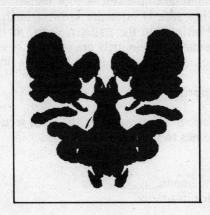

    a. The Jackson Pollock in your firm's main conference room.
    b. A hit-and-run victim—and potential client.
    c. The insanity defense.
    d. Your kitchen linoleum.
    e. Prefer to research the issue before commenting.

13. If you were to drive over a dog that had darted into the street, your first impulse would be to:
    a. Feel concern that it might still be alive and suffering.
    b. Roll up your window.
    c. Try to locate the owner, to express your regret.
    d. Try to locate the owner, to demand payment for the dent in your grill.
    e. Back up and go over it again, to teach it a lesson.

14. During idle moments you fantasize about:
    a. Winning a multimillion-dollar class action against the American Medical Association.
    b. Oral arguments before the Supreme Court.
    c. Oral acts with the women in the *Sports Illustrated* swimsuit issue.
    d. Joining a big-city law firm, so you wouldn't have any more idle moments.

SCORING YOUR ANSWERS

1. (a) 0 (b) 1 (c) 2 (d) 7
2. (a) 0 (b) 1 (c) 2 (d) 7
3. (a) 1 (b) 1 (c) 6 (d) 2
4. (a) 5 (b) 3 (c) 1 (d) 7 (e) 4
5. (a) 4 (b) 0 (c) 1 (d) 2 (e) 0
6. (a) 1 (b) 3 (c) 4 (d) 6
7. (a) 0 (b) 2 (c) 2 (d) 7
8. (a) 7 (b) 6 (c) 6 (d) 0
9. (a) 0 (b) 3 (c) 4 (d) 7
10. (a) 3 (b) 5 (c) 2 (d) 0
11. (a) 0 (b) 4 (c) 6 (d) 7
12. (a) 0 (b) 6 (c) 3 (d) 1 (e) 7
13. (a) 0 (b) 3 (c) 1 (d) 6 (e) 4
14. (a) 7 (b) 5 (c) 1 (d) 6

EVALUATING YOUR RESULTS

If you scored—

Between 65 and 93

Congratulations—sort of. You're compulsive, calculating, avaricious, sexually repressed, and no doubt already too blind to go out without a dog. You could make a real name for yourself in the law.

Between 45 and 64

Not bad. You have the makings of a lawyer, maybe even partnership material. Sometimes you let your feelings for humanity interfere with your professional role, but with work you could learn to repress these feelings.

Between 20 and 44

Hey, so you're not going to be the next Clarence Darrow. You're a likable person with a bright life ahead of you. Enjoy!

Between 0 and 20

You've gone too far the other way. You're a no-count, weak-kneed, mush-mouthed jellyfish without any gumption. Get your act together and try to make something of yourself—but not in the law.

CHAPTER TWO

GETTING INTO THE RIGHT LAW SCHOOL

"My roommate the Moonie scored in the 98th percentile on the LSAT and got into Harvard. Why didn't I?"

⚖

Neither law schools nor their admissions officers care about the whole person. Law school isn't college. It isn't out to mold you into a better human being or prepare you for life. It doesn't care whether any of your classmates will like you.

Sure, you swam the English Channel in ski boots and play classical ukulele. You managed the varsity jazzercise team, and you were the first male in your school's history to play Lady Macbeth. But law schools need more Junior Achievers like the *Titanic* needed more ice machines.

Law schools look at two factors: grades and LSAT scores. They just plug the figures into a formula and take as many applicants as they have room for (discounted by the number of people who will die, go to other schools, or decide there must be a less painful way to gird one's loins for life).

What about those stupid essays and recommendations required by the application? These represent ways of weeding people out, not bringing them in. Your essays might show you to be barely literate, notwithstanding your magna cum laude En-

The ivy-covered halls of the Harvard Law School

glish thesis at Princeton, "Over 100 Really Good Knock-Knock Jokes." Your recommendations might say only that your methadone treatment appears to be working.

The competition today is truly awesome. In 1990, over 100,000 people took the LSAT, with some 800 earning a *perfect* score (compared to 210 in 1989). Law school applications are being buoyed by *L.A. Law*—which is ironic, since it resembles real law about as much as Perry "I've never even had a case go to a jury" Mason.

Another contributing factor: the decline of Michael "All the money in the world can't make hair grow" Milken, Ivan Boesky,

Sir William Blackstone— would his LSAT score get him into law school today?

and other Wall Street glitterati. Today's young-and-greedy are returning to the law.

But take heart: The number of spaces available is similarly awesome. There are 175 ABA-accredited law schools in this country—176 if you count the U.S. Army Judge Advocate General's School (which nobody does). And some of the best schools have the most spaces: Harvard has over 1,600 students in its basic J.D. program; Georgetown has over 2,000. Any literate primate in the country can get in somewhere.

Still, if you won't be happy unless you get into a name-brand school, your best strategy is to go for the highest grades and LSAT scores you can get. There may be some well-rounded, likable people in law school, but that isn't what got them there.

The LSAT

There is ongoing debate as to what the Law School Admission Test measures beyond your ability to come up with some $50 to register and several No. 2 pencils. Nevertheless, experience shows that two factors may significantly enhance your performance during the hour of truth: (1) familiarity with the style of LSAT questions, and (2) a good supply of antidiuretics. The latter can be obtained at any drugstore. The former can be had from the following sample questions.

Sample LSAT Questions

A. READING COMPREHENSION

DIRECTIONS: Read each passage below and answer the multiple-choice questions that follow.

1. "It was the best of times, it was the worst of times, it was the age of wisdom, it was the age of foolishness [you now have two minutes to read the novel *A Tale of Two Cities,* attached to your exam booklet] . . . it is a far, far better rest that I go to than I have ever known."

   QUESTION: In the above novel, what time is it?
   a. The best of times.
   b. The worst of times.
   c. *The New York Times.*
   d. About two o'clock.

2. "Know thyself."

   QUESTION: In the above passage, the writer is:
   a. Plagiarizing Plato.
   b. Employing an archaic usage.
   c. Advocating a solipsistic approach to epistemology.
   d. Describing your social life.

B. ANALYTICAL REASONING

DIRECTIONS: In this section you are given a multiple-choice question based on a stated set of conditions.

1. Einstein's theory of relativity postulated that there can be no motion at a speed greater than that of light in a vacuum, and time is dependent on the relative motion of an observer measuring the time. If a hydrogen atom electron is accelerated at a rate of π^2/speed of light through an inverse hypermagnetic positron field and then bombarded with neutrons from a nuclear/hemorrhoidal pile in a critical core reaction, what time is it?
   a. The best of times.
   b. The worst of times.
   c. Time to think about business school.
   d. About two o'clock.

2. For a dinner party, Missy must prepare several different three-bean salads, using chili beans, wax beans, lima beans, kidney beans, soybeans, and garbanzos. Note that (a) wax beans and lima beans do not taste good together, (b) kidney beans and soybeans do not look good together, and (c) chili beans and refried beans will render you incapable of holding solid food.

   Missy can prepare how many salads of the following types:
   a. Seven that resemble the bottom of a bird cage.
   b. Four that will have her guests exchanging embarrassed glances within ten minutes.
   c. Three that her pet goat would not eat.
   d. None of the above. If you want to be a bean counter, take the CPA exam.

C. LOGICAL REASONING

DIRECTIONS: In this section you are required to evaluate the reasoning of the given passages.

1. If Mr. Smith is a member of Club A, and Ms. Johnson is a member of Club B, and Mr. Smith and Ms. Wilson are members of Club C, and no members of Club B who are also members of Club A are women who belong to the same club as men who belong to more than one club, *then:*
   a. Mr. Smith is a lesbian.
   b. Club B must be in California.
   c. Ms. Johnson lied about her vasectomy.
   d. About two o'clock.

2. Ramona said, "All dogs bark. This animal does not bark. Therefore this animal is not a dog."
   Which of the following most closely parallels the logic of the foregoing syllogism?
   a. Cats do not bark. Cats climb trees. Trees have bark.
   b. Lawyers overcharge. Taxi meters overcharge. Lawyers are taxi meters.
   c. George sells cars. Every car sold by George falls apart. George is a Chrysler dealer.
   d. Dogs bay at the moon. Your dates bay at the moon. You would be better off getting to know thyself.

D. EVALUATION OF FACTS

DIRECTIONS: In this section you are required to apply the stated rules to a given factual situation:

RULES: The offense of murder consists of (1) a deadly act against a human being, and (2) an intent to commit the deadly act.

FACTUAL SITUATION: Gary, a Rosicrucian zeppelin mechanic, enters Sydney's Unisex Barbershop in a tough section of Beverly Hills. While he is waiting for a shampoo, an employee of Sydney's Unisex Barbershop sees him and, believing him to be someone else, runs a chain saw through the upper half of his head.

QUESTION: On trial for murder, the employee of Sydney's Unisex Barbershop should be found:

a. Clearly guilty of taking too much off the top.
b. Not guilty because of assumption-of-risk principles respecting unisex barbershops.
c. Guilty but nevertheless qualified for the Los Angeles Police Department.
d. About two o'clock.

CHAPTER THREE

LAW SCHOOL

"Are You Telling Me Socrates Did It This Way?"

⚖

The Law School Experience

Legal lore describes the law school experience thus:

First year, they scare you to death.

Second year, they work you to death.

Third year, they bore you to death.

This is roughly accurate. The most memorable aspect of the first year—fear—is the result of the *Socratic method* of instruction, or "learning through humiliation." (More on this below.)

For a number of you, this year will also offer several substantial gratifications, including learning how our legislative and judicial systems really work,

mastering a new and rigorous intellectual discipline, enjoying English at its most precise and elegant, by the likes of Holmes and Brandeis, and getting your foot in the door of a still elite, professional club.

The overwork in the second year is the result of insecurity. Based on first-year grades, only 10 percent of the class now ranks in the top 10 percent of the class—a phenomenon which may have been anticipated by the more reflective among you.

Law school has been described as a place for the accumulation of learning: First-year students bring some in. Third-year students take none away. Hence, it accumulates.

But 100 percent of the class is *used* to ranking in the top 10 percent. Those who now make up the bottom 90 percent feel confused and anxious—even desperate. Consistent with the modus operandi that got them into law school in the first place, they channel these feelings into hard work.

As for the boredom in the third year, you would have noticed this in the second year if you hadn't been so scared.

THE SOCRATIC METHOD

Is Hemlock the Only Escape?

The most talked-about aspect of the law school experience is the Socratic method of instruction, featured prominently in *The Paper Chase, One L,* and *The Silence of the Lambs.* Designed to convey not bare information but a distinctive *method* of analysis, it involves an exchange or dialogue between the professor and a randomly chosen student, with the student pressed to answer ever deeper levels of questions regarding the case or issue of the day.

The Socratic method is controversial. Its potential pedagogic value indisputably surpasses that of the old-fashioned lecture method, which caused even diligent students to experience symptoms of narcolepsy. In practice, however, its shortcomings are severe.

First, few professors are adept in its use. The skills of a few recognized masters—Philip Frickey of U. Minnesota, David Sokolow of U. Texas, Socrates of U. Athens—cannot offset the ineptness of those who waste innumerable class hours thus:

PROFESSOR WEYMOUTH: Ms. Gratz, are you with us today?

STUDENT GRATZ *(raising hand)*: Here.

PROFESSOR WEYMOUTH: Then let us proceed. What am I thinking?

STUDENT GRATZ: I beg your pardon?

PROFESSOR WEYMOUTH: What thought is passing through my mind at this moment?

STUDENT GRATZ: Uh . . . I don't exactly know . . . it could be any . . . that is, I'm not—

PROFESSOR WEYMOUTH: Ms. Gratz, did you manage to overlook the assignment I gave at the end of the class yesterday?

STUDENT GRATZ: No! I read it— twice, in fact. It involved the Supreme Court's interpretation of Section 805(b) of the National Labor Relations Act.

PROFESSOR WEYMOUTH: If you've read it, *as you claim,* why are you unable to answer a simple question regarding the NLRA?

FAMOUS PEOPLE YOU WOULD NEVER
HAVE GUESSED WENT TO LAW SCHOOL

*The universe of lawyers boasts not only a dazzling roster of persons
famous for their contributions to the law, but also
a colorful cast of characters distinguished in other ways:*

*Howard Cosell—
toupee model,
sportscaster*

*Leo Tolstoy—gentleman farmer,
author*

*Mahatma Gandhi—
weaver, politician*

*Archibald MacLeish—
bohemian, poet*

*Warren Burger—
Chief Justice of
Supreme Court*

The other practical problem with the Socratic method is that professors who are either lazy or uninterested in teaching use it to kill class time without having to prepare a lecture:

PROFESSOR RYAN: Mr. Cane, what did you think of the cases assigned for today?

STUDENT CANE: All of them? They were fine, I guess. Are you thinking of any one in particular?

PROFESSOR RYAN: Take any one you like. Did you agree or disagree with it?

STUDENT CANE: Well, there was one I can think of that I agreed with.

PROFESSOR RYAN: Okay. Let's see, uh, Mr. Feder, do you agree or disagree with the case to which Mr. Cane is referring?

STUDENT FEDER: I'm not sure. Which one is he referring to?

PROFESSOR RYAN: Mr. Cane, please explain the case to which you're referring to Mr. Feder.

This sort of thing is a far cry from the system that produced Plato. If Socrates were alive today, he'd be turning over in his grave.

Just because a professor calls on you doesn't mean you have to answer. If the professor doesn't know you personally (most won't) or have a seating chart with pictures (many will), you can simply remain silent—the "foxhole technique"—and pretend you're not there.

The only problem with this is that students who know you may give you away by glancing in your direction. If this happens, turn and stare at the person sitting beside you.

Law Students and Law Professors

The Good, the Bad, and the Neurotic

Law students have to learn to deal with two sets of people: classmates and professors. The former have to be dealt with because they're physically ubiquitous—in the classroom, at the campus cafeteria, on that obscure library sofa where you were hoping to take a nap. The latter have to be dealt with because they're *psychologically* omnipresent, hovering about like superegos that speak in Latin.

LAW STUDENTS

Although your fellow law students will come in all sizes, colors, pedigrees, and genders, they will fall into a few easily identifiable categories.

The Mainstreamer

Most of your classmates will have proceeded directly from college to law school and will be planning to go directly into private practice—sort of like the great Tinkers-to-Evers-to-Chance double-play combination, only

here it's B.A. to J.D. to C.A.S.H. —and maybe to D.O.A.

Some will have chosen this path out of driving ambition. Others will have been forced into it by their parents. Most will have done it because they couldn't think of anything else to do.

If male, the Mainstreamer's attire is conventional, his hair length short, his politics moderate to conservative, and his drug habits mild. If female, her dress is conventional, her politics mildly feminist, her parents somewhat anxious about her future, and her willingness to engage in premarital sex dependent upon whether the relationship is "meaningful."

By and large, you will be able to understand and enjoy these people. The odds are that you are one of them.

The Grad School Burnout

A number of your classmates will have spent time working on other graduate degrees before going into law. Usually the Grad School Burnout switched fields out of simple necessity: She abandoned Hobbes for Holmes, Blake for Blackstone, and Proust for Prosser because she was in the habit of eating.

The Grad School Burnout has a hint of pathos about her, because she sees all too clearly that what would have been the next generation of philosophers, historians, and scientists has been transmogrified into an army of litigators, patent attorneys, and corporate proofreaders. Don't feel too sorry for the Grad School Burnout, however; she may be broke, but she represents strong competition.

The Computerhead

The primary distinguishing feature of the Computerhead is that his undergraduate major was physics, engineering, or some other "hard" science. You can still recognize him by his thick glasses and the pocket calculator that he keeps strapped to his waist—even when he sleeps.

In college, traveling under the label of Nerd, the Computerhead hung around the computer center on Saturday nights to meet women. He did this for four years, even though he never met any.

The Flamer

Flamers, known in some schools as "Gunners," are the most conspicuous as well as the most objectionable feature of law school. Flamers will have their hands in the air throughout all classes, manually pleading for an opportunity to discuss arcane points of law discovered in unrequired reading. At the end of each class they will bolt from their seats (consistently front and center) to the podium, where they will collar the professor and further attempt to display their mastery of the obscure.

The psychology of the Flamer is pitiable. Deeply anxious and insecure, he degrades himself regularly with brown-nosing of authority figures—not just professors but law librarians, weekend security guards, and the director of campus food services. The important fact for you to remember is that the Flamer's tactics reflect his internal ne-

The Computerhead

LAW SCHOOL BINGO

This is one of law school's most entertaining pastimes, and Flamers deserve the credit. Before class someone distributes sheets with the names of the most obnoxious Flamers laid out in a grid, like numbers on a Bingo card. Each sheet is different. As given Flamers raise their hands and are called on, you cross their names off on your sheet. Whoever gets three in a row calls out "Bingo!"—thus becoming entitled to the prize of the day.

A word to the wise: If yours is ever the waving hand whose recognition by a professor triggers a cry of "Bingo," followed by titters and perhaps a few murmurs of disappointment, give some serious thought to whether your classroom conduct would benefit from a touch of restraint.

cessities, *not* the realities of the law school situation. The Flamer is no more likely to get good grades than you are.

You cannot always ignore the Flamer; his excesses force their way into your life. But you should resist the temptation to suture a dog muzzle to his face. Professors know how to deal with Flamers, having encountered them before. Flamers are as old as the law.

LAW PROFESSORS

Law professors are a proudly idiosyncratic lot. Being as weird as you want to be is a major perk of academia, and some law professors make Edward Scissorhands look conventional (and

Pete Rose handsome). Nevertheless, like their students, law professors fall into identifiable categories.

The National Expert

Most law faculties have at least one National Expert, someone whose name is associated across the land with a given subject—Williston on Contracts, Weinstein on Evidence, Yudkowitz on Brain Death. ("The main difference between 'brain' death and 'regular' death is that with the latter you're not guaranteed a job with the post office.")

There is only a chance correlation, if any, between status as a National Expert and competence as a teacher. The National Expert didn't attain that status by devoting lots of time to teaching. Her lectures consist of "cases I have won" and "Supreme Court Justices I call by their first names."

Many National Experts are wealthy. Those with expertise in tax, securities, and other commercial areas maintain lucrative consulting practices in the "one day per week" to which their teaching contracts purport to restrict such activities.

National Experts in noncommercial areas such as civil procedure or federal courts convert their expertise into BMWs by publishing $57.50 casebooks that their classes are required to purchase.

The Fuzzhead

Some professors specialize in areas of notable obscurity. The Fuzzhead teaches undersubscribed seminars on "Noise Regulation Under Navajo Tribal Law" or "Agricultural Sewage and Meadow Muffin Disposal Under the Environmental Protection and Disgusting Accumulations Act."

The Fuzzhead (possibly a Computerhead in law school) may be brilliant, but the same escapist impulses that got him into his area of expertise render him unable to relate to other warm-blooded bipeds. He is a consistently miserable teacher, particularly when required to teach mainstream courses such as Contracts or Evidence. He should be avoided unless he is an easy grader—or unless you are of the Fuzzhead ilk yourself.

The Old Curmudgeon

The Old Curmudgeon is a classic feature of the law school landscape. Sometimes a former National Expert grown irascible in his twilight years, he is dogmatic, demanding, impatient, crotchety, and surly—on a good day.

The Old Curmudgeon conducts his classes as would a drill sergeant: You *will* attend all of his classes, you *will* be in your seat when he arrives at the beginning of each, you *will* be prepared to discuss any assigned case.

The only way to deal with the Old Curmudgeon is craven capitulation. If he accuses you of inadequate preparation, shamefacedly apologize. If he charges you with genetic idiocy, lament your forebears' reprehensible tradition of inbreeding.

Take comfort in the knowledge that the humiliation you risk by entering his class every day is no greater than that risked by each of your classmates. Take additional comfort

The Old Curmudgeon

in the knowledge that the Old Curmudgeon may not last another semester.

The Young Star

Law school faculties are in constant search of the Young Star, someone short on years but long on the right credentials. Usually a former Supreme Court clerk and law review editor-in-chief, the true Young Star confirms her Young Stardom by early publication of a highly ac-

claimed article or treatise, one noted for its "fresh outlook," "novel insights," and proposals for reform that will get about as far off the ground as the Stealth Bomber.

The Young Star is a colorful figure on the law school campus, with her grubby clothes, longshoreperson's vocabulary, and self-rolled funny cigarettes at parties. Also colorful are her apocalyptic analyses of society. The only people who agree with these analyses are undergraduates, but their support is sincere.

The Deadwood

Every law student faculty has a few tenured members who don't do anything. In this respect law school faculties resemble private firms.

Although not necessarily elderly, Deadwoods don't write articles, don't serve on law-reform committees, don't engage in private consulting, and apparently don't prepare for their classes. No one is sure what Deadwoods do with their time. Rumor has it that some of them have very nice gardens.

The Entertainer

Many law school professors pride themselves on being entertaining. Some were irritated that Jay Leno was chosen over them to replace Johnny Carson. Because it is more fun to be entertained than bored as you sit in class, you will appreciate the Entertainer's antics.

The problem with the Entertainer is not so much that he wastes class time, although many Entertainers do, but that students are lulled by his levity into thinking he is an easy grader, only to get their socks blown off by the final exam. Enjoy the Entertainer, but don't slack up in his class any more than in your others. Tape your socks up for his final exam.

Law School in a Nutshell: The Hornbook's Hornbook

Law students overestimate the importance of good grades. You don't need good grades. You don't even need mediocre grades. History suggests, in fact, that you can be at the bottom of your class, an embarrassment to your school, so dumb that all you need for survival is medium light and watering twice a week—and still have reasonable prospects of becoming vice-president of the United States.

But we've always known it's better to be lucky than smart. The question is, what to do if you're not very lucky? Few law students are, and most compensate by going after their courses like demons (not necessarily a bad idea; see "The Résumé," page 000). They spend every waking hour trying to ingest, in readily upchuckable form, everything there is to know about certain "core" subjects.*

Students also study a number of non-core subjects, things

---

*Many students attempt to ingest these materials at the same time they are ingesting their breakfast or lunch. Keep in mind that dried oat bran, peanut butter, and the like on your textbooks substantially reduce their resale value.

that are silly (Cow Law), impractical (Law in Literature), or downright nonexistent (International Law). They do this either to pad their schedules or because they go to Yale and that's all that was offered.

But the core subjects dominate the first year, and they're all that a practicing lawyer needs to know. The following sections set forth all the concepts and buzzwords of these subjects in clearer form than you'd ever get in school.

CONTRACTS

The Ties That Bind

A passing familiarity with the law of contracts is all you need to hold yourself out as a "commercial" lawyer. Leases, security agreements, trust indentures, and lots of other documents with highfalutin names are just contracts. This is good to know if another lawyer presents you with some document and you have no idea what it is. If it requires signing and it isn't either a will or something that has to be filed in court, you can call it a "contract" without fear of being laughed at.

Offer and Acceptance

The entire law of contracts can be summed up in two words: offer and acceptance (well, three words).

An offer is just what it sounds

like: "Hey, baby, fifty bucks for some action?"

So is an acceptance: "Sure. Your place or mine?"

Whether a contract has been formed depends on whether there has been a "meeting of the minds." The acceptance must "match" the offer.

Craig offers to take Kim to an expensive place for dinner if she'll accompany him to the prom on Saturday night. Kim replies, "Not on your life, spittoon-face."

Here there has been no meeting of the minds. Kim's reply did not match Craig's offer. No contract was formed.

Both offers and acceptances can be conditional:

Andy: "I'd be honored to take you to the prom on Saturday night—*as long as* your face doesn't break out."

Betty-Jo: "Okay, *unless* someone else—*anybody* else—asks me to go."

Consideration

Complicating the law of contracts is the concept of "consideration." The law will not enforce just any promise. For example, it will not enforce a promise to make a *gift*: "The next time I see you I'm going to give you a knuckle sandwich." It will enforce only those promises given in exchange for some return promise or equivalent sacrifice. This return promise or sacrifice constitutes the consideration supporting the enforceability of the contract.

No one understands this concept. Why they call it consideration, when it has nothing to do with being nice to someone, is one of the law's well-shrouded mysteries.

Nevertheless, at least nominal consideration always has to be there. According to law school lore, the delivery of a mere peppercorn would be sufficient consideration for a contract to transfer the Empire State Building, complete with Fay Wray and a large hairy doorman who swats airplanes. This is why even multibillion-dollar contracts may start out with a bizarre recital: "For $1.00 and other valuable *consideration,* we the undersigned hereby agree . . ."

At the closing of the deal one of the lawyers may actually present the other with a one-dollar bill (promptly recording it and billing it to the client with interest).

Breach

What if your client breaches a contract? What if *you* breach a contract? Should either of you be embarrassed about it? Should your parents make you go through with it?

Not necessarily. In some instances the law *wants* you to breach your contract. Suppose you've entered a contract to build a house for someone on a piece of land that turns out to have a body of water about the size of, say, the Pacific Ocean two feet below the surface. The ground is so soft you couldn't pitch a pup tent on it, much less a building.

Do you have to proceed according to plan, however futile it may be? No. The law doesn't see any point in your going broke, getting upset, and having your face break out because of this one contract.

All the law would require is that you give the other fellow enough money to "make him whole." In deciding what would make him whole, a jury would take into account such factors as the cost of building the house elsewhere, whether either party knew about the water under the land, and the race and religion of the persons involved.

Unenforceable Contracts

The law won't enforce certain categories of contracts, regardless of the presence of consideration, the absence of breach, or anything else. One of these categories consists of contracts that are "contrary to public policy." Shylock's pound-of-flesh bargain would not be enforced north of the Mason-Dixon line today (southern jurisdictions remain very strict), and most courts would not require the loser of a bet on the Duke–U.N.L.V. basketball game to run three times around the U.N.L.V. campus shouting "Tark the Shark has hair!"

The same is true for contracts made "under duress." A court would not require you to perform a contract that you accepted after a fellow whose last name ends in a vowel made you an offer you couldn't refuse.* Of course, few such contracts actually make it to court, and there's no predicting how a judge will rule after receiving an offer to go swimming in the East River in a cement bathing suit.

A final category of unenforceable contracts involves "contracts of adhesion." Occasionally a judge decides that a given contract is so unfair, so grossly one-sided, that she'll be damned if she'll enforce it. The theory seems to be that no sane and sober person would sign such a contract, and the stronger party must have somehow duped the weaker. The term "contract of adhesion" comes from the idea that the judge "sticks up for you" despite the actual terms of the contract.

A classic case in this area involved a couple who bought a used Plymouth from a car dealer in New Jersey. The bill of sale carried a disclaimer—in print so small it could be read only with an electron microscope— saying that neither the dealer nor Chrysler would be liable for bodily injuries resulting from defects in the car. Supposedly the couple were stuck with that contract, but when the steering

wheel came off in the hands of the wife ten days later, she sued.

The judge ruled for the wife, saying the contract was unconscionable (which is bad, even for a lawyer). He said the average consumer has too little bargaining power in relation to the automobile giants, and the public interest in preventing bodily harm weighs against enforcing this kind of deal.

Liberals hail this judge as a righteous dude. Conservatives denounce him as just one more do-gooder venting his sexual frustrations on productive elements of society.

The liberals are right. This contract wasn't made between two rational, free-acting parties. No one in his right mind would buy a used Plymouth from a car dealer in New Jersey.

The preceding case doesn't mean you should get rid of all those unconscionable, illegible disclaimers in your own contracts. These provisions serve an important "dust in the eyes" function, blinding the other party to his actual rights.

Go ahead and include a paragraph saying the purchaser acknowledges having test-driven the car, inspected the spare tire, and counted the spark plugs, even though he won't have done any of that. Add a provision to the effect that the purchaser supervised the assembly of his stereo, even though the thing was

*If the offer came from a *lawyer* whose last name ended in a vowel, it was probably an offer you couldn't *understand*.

PALIMONY—
A TRAP FOR THE UN-WEARY

Except in a few special situations, contracts need not be in writing to be enforceable (although as a practical matter, oral contracts aren't worth the paper they're printed on). In some instances, contracts need not even be spoken to be enforceable; a court may find an "implied" contract based on the conduct of the parties.

Such contracts have received substantial publicity in recent years with the rise of "palimony" suits, usually brought by a woman against her former male lover (or "pal"), claiming breach of an implied contract of ongoing support. (There are also "galimony" cases, or suits by women against other women. We still await an appropriate label for suits by men against other men.)

There aren't a lot of statutes addressing this issue. It's basically a social question, one that turns on the mores of the day. What *are* the legitimate expectations of a woman who accepts an invitation to move in with a man for a couple of years? Has he necessarily promised her support for life? What if he invites her to stay over for a single evening—has he at least promised to treat her to brunch the next day?

What if the tables are turned—she's a rich radiologist and he's a starving artist who moves into *her* home? Does the whole thing depend on whether they had sexual relations? Should the result be different if he turns out to be impotent?

It's hard to counsel clients in this area, both because the law is in flux and because no would-be Lothario or Lothariette wants to double date with a lawyer.

For the present, the best way to ensure safe sex is to supply lecherous clients of all genders not only with condoms, but also with blank waiver forms (see sample next page), which they should have their prospective lovers execute at the first sign of lust—ideally before the first cocktail, and in any event before the Big Bang (a concept that has been discredited in astronomy, even as it persists in debauchery).

PALIMONY WAIVER

Date:_____
(If overnight,
be inclusive.)

The undersigned prospective lover ("The Lover"), being of sound mind, nubile body, and substantial libidinal urges, hereby acknowledges the mutual nature of all pleasures and gratifications arising from any present or foreseeable carnal relations, consummated or otherwise, between The Lover and

_____,
(client's name)

(said carnal relations being referred to hereinafter as "The Lust"), and hereby waives and disclaims any right(s) or entitlement(s) now owing in connection with, or hereafter arising from, The Lust, whether such right(s) or entitlement(s) are of a physical, mental, emotional, spiritual, existential, philosophical, subliminal, otherworldly, out-of-body, televised, or other nature.

_____
The Lover
(In Texas and Arkansas, it is legally sufficient to place The Lover's hoof or paw print on the reverse side of this form.)

put together in Taiwan. Throw in a clause in which the purchaser admits to having tested the video game on the premises of the store, even though he's an invalid who ordered the thing by phone.

The consumer won't be able to *find* these clauses much less know they're legally meaningless. When he comes back to complain that the car has no spark plugs, the stereo gets only one channel (twenty-four-hour static), and the video game makes the Mario Brothers look more like the Marx Brothers, you can show him these clauses, and he'll go away.

Then all you'll have to worry about is whether you're going to burn in hell for your sins.

CIVIL PROCEDURE

Avoiding the Merits of a Case

If you want to be a trial lawyer, you need to know about "civil procedure," which refers to the rules of court you must follow when suing someone or being sued. The word *civil* has nothing to do with politeness; it differentiates the rules that apply to a "civil" action from those that apply to a "criminal" action. That latter is what you'll face in most places if you stab someone, or if you jaywalk in Washington, D.C. (unless you happen to be carrying a pound of cocaine, in which case you'll be nominated for office).

Civil procedure is easy. You just read the rules for whatever court you happen to be dealing with and follow them like recipes in a cookbook: To start a lawsuit, you do A; to oppose a lawsuit, you do B. If the other side lies, you do X; if your side lies, you do Y.

Four concepts merit special attention.

Standing

"Standing" refers to a concrete, personal interest in a particular lawsuit. It's something you're required to have in order to

stay in court. Such an interest is easy to prove when you've been run over by a truck. Your broken legs give you standing.

But what if you want to sue Congress for passing a law restricting fat people from walking on public sidewalks during the lunch hour? If you're anorexic, you don't have standing, because the law in question doesn't affect you personally. Even dating a fat person isn't enough.

This explains why you often see six-year-old kids as the nominal plaintiffs in school-desegregation cases, or schizophrenic street people as the nominal plaintiffs in welfare litigation. They've been recruited by lawyers. They don't know what the hell those people in suits are yelling about, but they have standing.

Jurisdiction

The concept of jurisdiction relates to which courts can hear which cases. You can't always get your case into a federal court, for example, even though that Texas judge won't read your papers and hates you because you have a beard, or don't have a beard, or anything else he feels like holding against you.

To understand jurisdiction, just recall how things worked when you were a kid: "Cases" involving who got to use the family car probably fell within Dad's jurisdiction; those involving whose turn it was to do the dishes probably fell within Mom's. If it wasn't clear who had jurisdiction, you engaged in "forum shopping"—you went to the one most likely to give you the answer you wanted.

The basic jurisdictional rule is that everything goes into the state courts unless there's a special reason it should go into a federal court. Lawyers would generally *rather* have their cases in federal court, partly because the judges are better and the rules of the game a lot clearer, but mainly because of prestige. A lawyer who says, "I'm trying a case in *federal* court," is boast-ing. One who says, "I'm trying a case in *state* court," is telling you where she's trying her case.

The reason for the prestige of federal cases is that they involve more money. The reason for the extra money goes back to the nature of jurisdiction.

There are two ways a federal court can get jurisdiction over a case. The first involves somebody going up against a federal law, i.e., a law passed by Congress, as opposed to one passed by a city, a state, or the National Rifle Association.

A case involving a federal law usually involves a lot of money, because Congress only passes laws on important subjects, like requiring those "Do Not Remove" labels on your pillows and mattresses that always make you tear the fabric to get them off. Congress leaves minor things like murder and rape to the states.

The second way a federal court can get jurisdiction over a case involves the state citizenship of the parties to the lawsuit. If the plaintiff (the fellow with the tire tracks on his face) is from Alabama, and the defendant (the fellow who was driving the cement truck) is from New York, the two parties have "diversity of citizenship." The case can get into federal court as a so-called "diversity suit."*

*Not to be confused with the plaid suit, striped shirt, and paisley tie that your Uncle Pollard from Denver wears to church.

The theory behind this is that an Alabama jury might not take kindly to a New Yorker. The fact that no one takes kindly to a New Yorker is irrelevant. Supposedly the federal judge, appointed by the president, detests New Yorkers less than most people do, and he'll keep the Alabama jury from doing a bankrollectomy on the New Yorker.

Like cases involving federal laws, diversity suits tend to involve a lot of money—it costs more to run over somebody twelve states away than to run over your next-door neighbor. Hence the extra prestige of a federal case.

Service of Process

Long before you can begin to explain to a jury how you were sexually harassed by your lecherous boss, you have to give your boss notice of the lawsuit. She's entitled to defend herself.

You give her notice by delivering to her, or "serving" upon her, a copy of your complaint. This is called "service of process."

Service of process raises many practical questions. If you go to your boss's address and she won't open the door, how do you serve her? By placing it on her doorstep? Throwing it through her window? Beating her dog until she can't stand the pitiful howling and opens the door?

One option is to hire an independent agent to perform the service. A private process server, usually a former bar bouncer or mud wrestler, will lurk in the shadows of her home until he catches her, invariably scaring her into a coronary. (*See* Torts, below.)

The problem with private process servers is that they are not known for their reliability. The job doesn't pay that well, and not that many people enjoy lurking in the shadows of strangers' homes.

Private process servers are famous for tossing complaints into the nearest sewer—"sewer service." Then they report back to you for payment. Because private process servers outweigh

Mr. T—typical private process server

you by eighty pounds, you pay without question.

Class Actions

Contrary to what you might think, a "class action" is not an action between people who wear Gucci loafers, vacation at Saratoga, and seldom adorn their homes with bowling trophies. It is a lawsuit with lots of people on one side or the other.

Class actions are important to know about because they're incredibly lucrative for lawyers.

Consider a suit you might bring against ABC on behalf of viewers of "20/20" who came down with lockjaw after prolonged exposure to Barbara Walters: You sue for $10 million, settle for $2 million, and keep $500,000 for your fee—all without lifting a briefcase.

Class actions consistently involve a lot of money, as the people in a given class may number in the thousands, and they invariably settle before trial, because wealthy corporate defendants (carefully chosen by you after reviewing their bal-

---

SURE-FIRE CLASS ACTIONS

Some of the best class actions are still waiting to be brought. Consider the following sure-fire winners:

1. A suit against Quaker Oats on behalf of consumers of oat bran who now resemble Wilfred Brimley.
2. A suit against Milli Vanilli for damage to the reputations of talentless people everywhere.
3. A suit against Howard Johnson's on behalf of interstate motorists who sampled HoJo cola and then wrecked their cars while vomiting.
4. A suit against NBC on behalf of people who stayed up for "The Tonight Show" and didn't get Jay Leno.
5. A suit against *Cosmopolitan* on behalf of readers who still haven't achieved multiple ecstasy.
6. A suit on behalf of Volkswagen purchasers who later found out their cars were assembled in America.
7. A suit against William F. Buckley, Jr., on behalf of viewers of "Firing Line" who now speak with fake British accents and have become psychologically incapable of pumping their own gas.

ance sheets and income statements) know juries will stick it to them if given half a chance. Whenever a big class action settles, the lawyer goes home a wealthy individual.

The most famous class action involved a taxicab company in New York that had adjusted all its meters to charge illegally high rates, cheating thousands of people out of a few dollars each. Some lawyer filed a complaint on behalf of the "class" of cheated taxi passengers in Manhattan.

As this case made clear, class actions are not always simple affairs: How many people were cheated? Out of how much? Who were they? Don't all taxi drivers rip people off?

The bugs still haven't been worked out of class-action suits, but it's worth your while to stick with them. For plain old filthy lucre, a lawyer can't do better.

TORTS

Ambulance Chasing for Fun and Profit

If you plan to get wealthy as a litigator, you need to master "torts," as well as "civil procedure": Civil procedure tells you *how* to sue someone; torts tell you *what* to sue him *for*.

The first issue you need to

understand in the area of torts is, what *is* a tort?

If someone stabs you, there are three ways he could get into trouble. First, the government could prosecute him. Stabbing someone is a crime. It has been for years.

Second, if you and your assailant had previously exchanged promises not to stab each other, you could sue him for breach of contract. He *promised* not to do it.

Third, you could sue him for carving you up. You could demand payment for your medical bills, your pain and suffering, your prosthetic navel. What is the legal theory on which you could sue him? (You always need a theory.) He has committed a tort—in this case, the tort of redesigning your anatomical landscape without your consent.

A tort is any wrong you can sue someone for. Except breach

of contract—that's called breach of contract.

So, if the *government* takes the case to court, it's a *crime* (in all instances that you need to worry about). If *you* take it to court, and there was no breach of contract, it's a tort.

Once you've got a handle on what a tort is, all you have to do to bring a lawsuit is pick a tort, any tort. If you don't like the selection, feel free to make up your own (explaining it to the judge as a logical step in an already apparent trend in the law).

The One-Bite Rule:
Make that first bite count!

The One-Bite Rule

To get you going, consider a classic feature of tort law, the "one-bite rule." Normally a dog owner may allow his dog to run freely through the neighborhood. This is considered unobjectionable, because dogs are common domestic pets and usually don't bite people—unlike, say, hippopotamuses, which must be securely leashed.

What if your adorable Great Dane Gaylord rips a forty-stitch gash in your neighbor's right arm? Good old playful Gaylord—*you* know he was just being affectionate. But your crabby neighbor (now called "Lefty") is upset. Can Lefty sue you and win?

No. You were not *negligent.*

You had no reason to think Gaylord would bite anyone. You did not fail to act like that famous figure of tort law, the "reasonable person."

Lefty's gash is just his bad luck—like a tornado, flood, or rhino stampede.

But what about rabid dogs? They're *known* to bite people. What about that German shepherd as big as a Volkswagen that moved into the neighborhood just about the time your cat disappeared?

More important, what about *Gaylord,* now that he has "known vicious propensities"?

For such animals, judges developed the one-bite rule: After one bite, you're on notice that the animal is dangerous; and for every bite thereafter, you can be held liable.

The lesson from this is clear: Don't squander that first free bite. Make it count.

False Imprisonment

Another classic tort, a darling of law professors, is "false imprisonment." Contrary to what you might think, this doesn't refer to the situation in which policemen pounce on you, beat hell out of you, and then lock you up down at the station—all because they think you look like Zsa Zsa Gabor. (That's something else, including—if it happens in L.A.—routine.)

False imprisonment is what you sue young thugs for when they surround your car and won't let you out. False imprisonment could also be what your neighbor sues you for when Gaylord chases him up a tree and who't let him down until you call Gaylord home for dinner. The key is impairment of someone's freedom of movement.

Law professors love to pose the question: What if someone locks your door for several hours while you're asleep, so that you can't get out, but you don't *know* you can't get out. False imprisonment?

As an academic matter, who knows? Who cares? As a practical matter, if you have a client

to whom this has happened, go for it! The jurors will identify with the sleeping party and be incensed at the thought of someone hanging around outside the door. They'll think, "What if I woke up and had to go to the bathroom?"

Res Ipsa Loquitur

If you're going to get a jury to award you or your client money because of someone's tort, you of course have to convince them the tort actually happened. Usually you do this by eyewitness testimony: You get the guy who was sleeping off a bender in a nearby alley to swear your client had a green light when the bus hit him.

But what if there were no eyewitnesses? What if the bender guy is so far gone that he can't get the story straight? All is not lost—you resort to the doctrine of *res ipsa loquitur*. This is Latin for "the thing *(res)* speaks *(loquitur)* for itself *(ipsa)*."

Note that the words are out of order. No wonder Latin is a dead language.

The actual case that gave rise to this doctrine involved a fellow who was walking along one day, minding his own business, when out of the blue he was struck—right on the head—by a barrel of flour. He didn't see it coming. He didn't know where it came from. He just woke up in the hospital covered with flour and looking like the Pillsbury doughboy.

He sued the owner of the nearby building, insisting that the owner or one of his employees must have pushed the barrel out of the window. The problem was that the victim couldn't prove it. He hadn't seen anything.

He won anyway. The judge said that in some cases the negligence is so clear from the circumstances that proof isn't necessary. He said, "The thing speaks for itself." The only question is, why did he say it in Latin?

Proximate Causation

A final subject you need to understand if you're going to line your wallet on the basis of someone's tort is the concept of "proximate causation." Every event has millions of causes. Say your son Johnny is injured when he falls off the new bicycle you gave him for Christmas. Who or what *caused* his injury?

Did the bicycle company cause it by manufacturing a defective bike? Did the city cause it by failing to fill in those potholes that swallow buses whole? Did Gaylord cause it by leaping at Johnny with that "dinner time" look in his eyes? In theory, causation could be traced all the way back to Jesus of Nazareth for "causing" you to celebrate Christmas.

The judges who have addressed this subject say you have to identify the "proximate" cause of the event in order to assign liability. This doesn't resolve the problem, however. Of all the possible causes of your son's injury, only Jesus's birth can be excluded for not being a proximate cause—and plaintiffs' lawyers would concede that only because of the service-of-process problems involved.

The idea that each event has a proximate cause really doesn't help at all. It just gives judges a label to apply to whomever they want to stick with the cost of the accident. In this case, the judge would probably assign liability to the bicycle company. It has all the money. Who cares that the judge's wisdom and charity will make Johnny's younger brother's bike cost $10 more next Christmas?

REAL PROPERTY

Dirt and Things Thereon

Every lawyer should be familiar with the law of "real property."

For one thing, it's a jargon-filled area, requiring fluency in Latin and Olde English. When other lawyers try to intimidate you with terms like easement, seisin, and quitclaim, you need to know enough to be able to come right back at them with terms like caduceus, amanuensis, and hypothalamus. Besides, understanding real property law is the only way to keep that sleazy real estate agent from ripping you off on the purchase or sale of your house.

Real property comprises two categories of things: (1) land, earth, soil, dirt—everything along these lines except what your potted plant is sitting in and what accumulates between your toes after you've been wearing sandals awhile; and (2) "fix-tures," i.e., buildings and other items so large, heavy, and immobile as to be virtually part of the land. This latter category includes Caucasian basketball players and some of the people you meet through the personal ads.

Real property law is a game of labels. For example, if someone sells you an acre of farmland, and it's yours, and you can do with it whatever you want, you don't just say it's *your* land; you say that you hold a "fee simple absolute interest" in that land.

Suppose you want to give a favorite plot of land to your brother and his kids. (You hate your own kids. They bear an unsettling resemblance to the local tennis pro, whom the guys around the club refer to as Tyler the Wonder Horse.) Moreover, you want to make sure that it stays in your brother's family for as long as he has heirs.

In this case you don't just give your brother the deed with the restrictions scribbled on the back. You give him a "fee tail interest" in the land.

There are scores of these kinds of labels. They don't make sense. They don't sound like anything you've ever heard of. You just have to memorize them.

Consider the following rules that every law student must know by heart for his final exam in real property:

> Of the defeasible estates, the fee simple determinable, a.k.a. fee simple on a special limitation, creates a possibility of reverter in the grantor and an executory interest in the third person, whereas the fee simple subject to a condition subsequent creates a power of termination, a.k.a. right of entry, in the grantor, as well as an executory interest in the third person. The possibility of reverter is alienable, devisable, and descendable. In contrast, the power of termination is devisable and descendable but not capable of inter vivos transfer.

The astonishing thing is that every bit of the foregoing is absolutely true.

Squatters' Rights

A peculiar but important concept of real property law is that you can acquire valid legal title to a piece of land simply by taking it and holding onto it for a long time. This method of acquiring land is known as "adverse possession."

It isn't quite as easy as it sounds. First, you really have to *have* the land. The courts say your use and possession of it must be "actual." If you decided you'd like three feet of your neighbor's lawn to round out your croquet field, it's not enough just to *proclaim* that the three feet are yours. You have to put up your wickets and start playing.

Second, your use must be "open" and "hostile." You can't just hop onto the lawn at night, wearing dark clothes and sneakers, and have a friend snap a flash photo of you to prove you were there. And you can't sucker your neighbor by telling him you're just borrowing the space for a while, like a cup of sugar. You have to be claiming it's *yours*. Guard dogs and spring guns would help satisfy this requirement. Or a sign like the one on the Kennedy compound in West Palm Beach: TRESPASSERS WILL BE VIOLATED.

Third, your use of the land has to be "exclusive." If three

DEED

THIS DEED, made and entered into this 23rd day of May, 1626, by and between PETER MINUIT, Royal Governor of New Amsterdam, for and on behalf of the Empire of the Netherlands ("Purchaser"), and BUCOLIC BUFFALO, Chief, for and on behalf of the Carnarsee Native Americans ("Seller"):

WITNESSETH

That for and in consideration of trinkets and other schlock worth about SIXTY GUILDERS, or TWENTY-FOUR DOLLARS ($24.00), receipt of which is hereby acknowledged, and the pipe of peace having been smoked, and the Seller knowing squat about the future value of real estate, the Seller does hereby grant, bargain, sell and convey, with GENERAL WARRANTY of title, unto the Buyer all that certain parcel of turf situate in a land once thought to be India (Christopher Columbus knowing squat about geography), but now referred to (by the Buyer) as the New World, and being more particularly described as follows:

An island, eventually to be known as Manhattan, a.k.a. the Big Apple, a.k.a. The City, and soon to be paved over entirely with asphalt and rendered incapable of sustaining higher life, located approximately in the North Atlantic Ocean and bounded by the Hudson, Harlem, and East Rivers.

This conveyance is made subject to all liens, encumbrances, and rights-of-way of record, which the Buyer may at his discretion eliminate by eliminating the holders thereof, said holders just being natives, after all.

WITNESS the following signatures:

Peter Minuit
_____
PETER MINUIT

X *Bucolic Buffalo*   *by Peter Minuit*
_____
BUCOLIC BUFFALO

other neighbors are growing to-
matoes on the turf you're trying
to claim, you lose.

Fourth, you have to use the
land "continuously." If you want
it so badly, and you're too cheap
to pay for it, cancel your world
cruise. Scratch your tour of duty
with the French Foreign Legion.
Definitely stay out of any branch
of the American military. You
have to *be* there.

Finally, you have to hold the
land and satisfy all these other
requirements for *twenty years*.
This is the hard part. This is
what keeps you from pitching
tent on your neighbor's lawn
with the idea of fighting him
off tooth and nail until title
changes hands—this and the
fact that if he calls the police,
they'll throw you in the slam-
mer for trespass.

If you could fulfill all these
requirements—it has happened
twice in the last four hundred
years—your neighbor's lawn
could be yours. You could
leave him singing the adverse-
possession blues.

With this information and a
bit of patience, you could take
over North Dakota. How do you
think the duPonts got Delaware?

The Rule Against Perpetuities

The most irritating feature of
real property law is the Rule
Against Perpetuities. You know
that great piece of farmland in
Kentucky where your father
grew up? Or that wonderful par-
cel of undisturbed beachfront
turf in Big Sur where you've
vacationed for years and that
you want to make sure stays in
the family forever? You can't
do it. The Rule Against Perpetuities won't let you.

First announced in 1681 by
the celebrated William of Nottingham, the Rule Against Perpetuities provides as follows:

> A contingent future interest which,
> by any possibility, may not vest
> within twenty-one years after some
> life in being, is void in its inception.

The main point, according to
modern theologians, is that no
one should be able to control a
piece of land forever. William
of Nottingham might have wanted
his back-forty acres to remain
farmland until the end of time,
but his desires in 1681 should
not control the use of the land
today. Similarly, Butch of De-
troit might like the idea of his
two acres on the South Side
remaining a parking lot throughout eternity, but people in the
year 2500 should be able to
dump nuclear waste there if they
want to.

The Rule Against Perpetuities has inspired endless pages
of discussion. These pages would
have been more usefully employed on spools in Howard

Johnson's restrooms along I-95.

If you were studying the Rule Against Perpetuities in law school, your final exam would require you to apply it to a hypothetical such as the following:

> A makes a gift to B, for the life of C, remainder to D's heirs, so long as D has heirs, but if C's firstborn should be of another race, then to E's heirs for so long as B's grandchildren may reside in Cleveland, then to such heirs of B as may survive the then living residents of Staten Island.

You would have two minutes to answer this question.

LAW REVIEW

The heart of law school is studying for classes. There's a ton of material to read—some casebooks come with wheels—and anyone who tells you otherwise is yanking your chain. Nevertheless, law school does offer several other activities to help kill that worthless half hour between "Cheers" and "L.A. Law" on Thursday nights. The activity you hear the most about is Law Review.

At every law school, about ten percent of the top students

are invited to join the Law Review. These students are selected on the basis of grades, a writing competition, or—at Yale—romantic involvement with one or more of the current editors.

This is the highest honor a law student can come by. If you make Law Review, you'll be flooded with offers from the highest-paying, hardest-working sweatshops in New York City. You'll be able to sell your soul at the maximum rate.

Why do employers value the Law Review credential so highly? Because researching an issue in depth and then writing it up under close supervision is an invaluable thinking and writing experience? Yes—but no. That is, it can be all that, but what employers really like about it is that nothing else offers so much tedious, petty grunt work. Anyone who can put up with it has real potential for success in private practice.

What do law reviewers do? First you have to understand what a Law Review is. To its editors, it is a holy writing. (Just think of how Moslems view the Koran, or investment bankers the *Wall Street Journal*.) To everyone else, a Law Review is a magazine—run by law students and published four to eight times per year, depending on the school.* It consists of both student and professional pieces, whose merit is judged by their obscurity, lack of practical value, and ratio of footnotes to text (an acceptable ratio is ten to one).

Law Review "staffers" (second-year students) write the student pieces, called "Notes" or "Comments," and "citecheck" everything being published. (More on citechecking below.) Third-year students, including the Editor-in-Chief, the Articles Editor, and the Editor of Punctuation and Italics, run the operation. They choose the professional pieces and presume to edit them, and they instruct and ride herd on the staffers.

If you have a chance to join your school's Law Review, you should probably take it. It *is* a handy credential. More important, the Law Review usually has its own offices, which gives you someplace other than a locker in which to hang your hat, as well as a private place to study when exam mania and undergraduate groupies have rendered the library unfit for work. (This is by no means a categorical put-down of undergraduate groupies, who have their own, sometimes memorable role to play in the law school experience.)

---

*Curiously, there is rarely a correlation between the month designated on each issue and the month of actual publication. When such a correlation occurs, there is invariably a disparity between the *year* designated and that of publication.

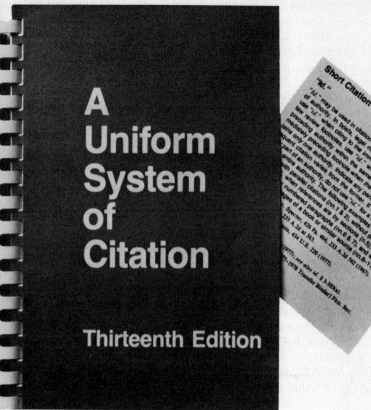

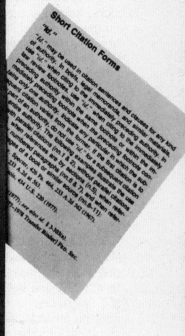

The Repository of Truth and Justice

LEGAL CITATION— THE BLUE BOOK

Confusing *supra* and *id* could cause an innocent person to go to jail and die.

Law reviewers spend the bulk of their time neither researching nor writing about the law, but "citechecking" the things they publish. There are two types of citechecking: "substantive," which means reviewing all the sources cited in a piece to make sure they actually say what the author says they say; and "technical," which means reviewing each citation for propriety of *style*. The latter is by far the more important.

The leading (and only) authority on legal citation style is a modest-looking but highly immodest paperback titled *A Uniform System of Citation,* commonly known as the Blue Book (from its color, which was once white, although people called it the Blue Book even then).

The Blue Book tells you which publications to italicize and when (Rule 1.1); which numerals to spell out and where (Rule 6.2); which periodicals to abbreviate and how (even in foreign languages—Rule 20.6). It tells you whether to leave a space between initials in personal names. (You don't: "W.C. Fields"— Rule 6.1(a).)

The Blue Book has expanded over the years—the twelfth edition ran 190 pages, the thirteenth 237, and the fourteenth 255, each new level of detail injecting an additional quantum of rigidity. In this respect the Blue Book could be said to resemble the very fluid of life —water—which expands as it hardens into ice. Other illuminating comparisons also spring to mind: The Blue Book is like a bucket of warm spit. It is like a moose turd pie. It is like the armpit of an infantryman after three months on field bivouac. One could go on and on.

The authors/editors of the Blue Book consist of law reviewers from four schools— Columbia, Harvard, Penn, and Yale. A few of these get together every four years to consider anew how many inside jokes they can squeeze into the minutiae of the Blue Book, which at this point is replete with references to friends, enemies, lovers, and pets (the last two frequently being the same) of many generations of law reviewers.

The bottom-line question: As long as citations are clear, why does anybody care about Blue Book style? Nobody does—except law reviewers and former law reviewers. For them, demonstrating Blue Book expertise is a way of letting other people know they were on the Law Review.

Blue Book Quiz

What really distinguishes a law reviewer from any other law student? His Blue Book expertise. He displays it proudly, a badge of honor, only too happy to instruct his inferiors on such questions as the citation of articles within articles collected in multi-volume, multiple-edition, foreign-language treatises.

You don't have to take that crap. You, too, can acquire the necessary Blue Book mastery to make you a leader of the profession. But first you need to know where you stand. Test yourself with the following quiz, which contains questions any self-respecting law reviewer could answer in his sleep. (Answers and a grading scale appear below.)

1. When citing the supplement to a state code, do you provide the date of the main volume?

2. How long must a passage be before you can quote it without quotation marks, just indenting it left and right?

3. For presidential proclamations, do you cite to the Code of Federal Regulations or the Federal Register?

4. When citing case names in briefs and legal memoranda, e.g., *Witzel* v. *Robertson,* do you underscore the *v* along with the names of the parties?

5. When citing an unenacted federal bill, do you cite to the session of Congress in which it was passed, or to the page of the *Congressional Record?*

6. When citing multiple subsections within a single statutory section, do you use one section symbol (§) or two (§§)?

7. For what books and pamphlets must you cite not only the date of publication but also the date of the original edition on which the modern edition is based?

8. What is the only part of the United States Constitution that must be capitalized?

9. In quotations, do you use ellipses to indicate language deleted from the beginning of a sentence?

10. What is the only item of punctuation incapable of being italicized?

QUIZ ANSWERS

1. Not unless a portion of the statute being cited appears in the main volume. Rules 3.2(c), 12.3(d).
2. Fifty words. Rule 5.1(a).
3. The C.F.R., if possible. Otherwise, to the Fed. Reg. Rule 14.7.
4. Yes. Rule 1.1(b).
5. Always the former; also the latter, if possible. Rule 13.2(a).
6. One. Rule 3.4(b).
7. Those published before 1870. Rule 15.4(c).
8. The Bill of Rights. Rule 8.
9. Not if the quoted language can stand by itself as a full sentence. Rule 5.3(i).
10. The period—usually; in some obscure forms of type, periods are square, in which case they *can* be italicized, by being tilted slightly. This isn't in the Blue Book, but law reviewers know it.

EVALUATING YOUR RESULTS

Correct Answers:

8–10 Advanced mastery. You'll

make an excellent associate at a large law firm.

5–7 Respectable; potential judge.

2–4 Seriously deficient. Be careful; you could wind up as a rain maker, rich and happy but not respected as a lawyer.

0–1 Not cut out for law. You'd be better off in a more productive sector of the economy—say, professional boxing.

CHAPTER FOUR

SUMMER CLERKSHIPS

Attend Summer Camp for Pay!

⚖

Many law students spend the summer after their second year of law school "clerking" at a firm. Summer clerkships are not unlike your high school prom, where you dressed like an adult, drank like an adult, and tried to fool around like an adult—only to learn later that it didn't come close to the real thing. Summer clerkships *resemble* private practice, but there are significant differences of which law students should be aware.

Socially, summer clerkships can be pleasant indeed. Most firms, particularly the large ones, wine and dine their summer clerks like visiting dignitaries. Your predecessors in the seventies and eighties enjoyed extravagances that today are available only through the Make-a-Wish Foundation, but you'll still be treated to a number of elegant meals and other outings designed to generate a serious lust for lucre in the corruptible heart of the typical law student.

This routine contains elements of the comical and the fraudulent. It is comical because of the disparity between the actual contribution of the clerks to the work of the firm and the attention accorded them: Few summer clerks do enough useful work to really pay their way, and *no* summer clerks actually command the respect of the senior partners.

It is fraudulent simply because it is unrealistic. To be sure, it happens every summer

Essentials tools for a summer clerkship

without fail. But the conviviality and gregariousness do *not* continue through the fall, winter, and spring. It is a seasonal phenomenon, and its focus is narrow. A summer clerk would do well to ask himself why that senior partner who strolls through the library says hello to him but not to the full-time associates. Does the partner not remember the associates' names? Did he know their names when they were summer clerks? Did something change when they signed on permanently?

Most law students save a few weeks at the end of the summer to travel or work on their tans. This is understandable but unfortunate, because that is when you could get your most realistic look at a firm. By then the firm's regulars are sick of playing up to the presumptuous little snots, and the facade of rah-rah enthusiasm collapses. The result is normalcy—grim, ugly normalcy.

If possible, stick around a while longer (and save your money for a real vacation at semester break)—it'll be an eye-opener.

Professionally, as well as socially, summer clerkships depart from reality. Most firms engage in "cream skimming," i.e., reserving for summer clerks all the interesting projects around the office (a big firm may have two or three in a summer). This is why so many summer clerks are later surprised to find that their positions as full-time associates offer all the dignity and satisfaction of cleaning up Madison Square Garden after the International Horse Show.

In more prosperous times, when the demand for young associates exceeded the supply, firms compounded the fraud by letting slide a lot of mistakes by summer clerks that if committed by a full-time associate would mean the loss of her job, or even her dictaphone. Firms still do this for law reviewers from the top law schools—such is the snobbery of the profession —but this is a mixed blessing, at best.

If you're not told of your shortcomings, if you're told only that your work was fine, you made a lot of friends, and everyone is eager to have you back, you are likely (wherever you end up) to persist in the patterns and practices that seemed to serve you so well, only to discover—after the black marks are on your record—that those patterns and practices are about as acceptable as white socks.

TO SPLIT OR NOT TO SPLIT

More and more law students are splitting their summers, spending one half of the summer at one firm and the other half at another, usually in two remote places (say, Wall Street and Midtown). The obvious benefit is that a student gets to check out two firms in a single summer, as well as romp across the country at someone else's expense.

Law firms don't like splits. They tolerate them only because competition for the top students forces them to do so. A split prevents the firm from scrutinizing the clerk as closely as it would like. Also, at the end of a split, the clerk usually has offers from two firms rather than one, so he doesn't feel compelled to return to the first one just because it's familiar and he can find the restroom there without a map.

Should a clerk split? Yes. Although it can be a bit of a hassle to find new digs in a strange city in the middle of the summer, the difference between what you'd learn about a firm in a full summer and what you can learn about it in a half summer doesn't begin to offset the informative value of looking at two different places.

Some law firms will try to scare you out of splitting. They'll tell you of one clerk or another who screwed up early on and then, because he was splitting, didn't have time to redeem himself and salvage an offer.

In most instances a clerk who has screwed up that badly couldn't resurrect himself even if he were the lead player in the New Testament. He couldn't salvage an offer with six more *months,* much less six more weeks. Such a clerk is definitely better off putting his mistakes behind him and moving on to someplace where he'll enjoy a clean slate.

CHAPTER FIVE

THE BAR EXAM

Thousands of Morons Have Passed It—So Can You!

⚖

The first thing you will encounter upon graduation from law school is the bar exam. A few slackers postpone it until after their judicial clerkships, and people who go straight into teaching often indulge the hope of avoiding it forever. The wiser course is to bite the bullet and take it, if for no other reason than to be able to tell your parents you're finally equipped to get a job.

Passing the bar does not require extraordinary intelligence. If you doubt this, stroll down to the nearest courthouse and check out the first lawyer you meet.

Passing the bar does require one thing: a decent memory. This is because most of the rules covered are completely arbitrary.

Albert Einstein—Physicist. Failed New York bar twice.

For example, either you know the order of distribution of a limited partnership's assets in your state, or you don't. An ability to *think* is irrelevant. Albert Einstein failed the New York bar twice.

This brings us to the first of two rules for passing the bar:

Read the materials! The "materials" consist of two to four volumes that you can obtain from the bar-review course in your state* and that contain almost every point of law the exam might cover.

You needn't memorize every single page. Your goal is to pass, not to get the highest grade in the state. A high grade is of absolutely no benefit. For one thing, no one will ever know—not even you. You can't find out your score unless you fail.

"M.C.E." should be your guide: Minimum Critical Effort. The ideal grade is the lowest passing grade in the state.

You will hear stories of people who spent all summer at the beach, glanced at the bar materials the night before, and then breezed through the exam. These stories are in the same categories as *Cinderella*. You have to give it *something*.

What if you fail? Failing the bar is not the end of the world. It just feels that way.

Many bright people fail. Most

go on to become judges and members of Congress.

Still, failing is a drag. Not only do you have to shell out good money to undergo yet another round of trial by No. 2 pencil, but you'll be slogging across town for the review lectures in February, when your co-sufferers won't be wearing skimpy summer clothes and nice tans.

Also, the whole world will know. First, the local paper publishes the names of everybody who passed, and people pore over the list the same way they pore over the list from a major plane wreck, as interested in the names that *aren't* on it as in those that are.

Second, when the results come out, some idiot invariably roars down the hallway at your firm (you've started work by then) shouting, "I passed! I passed! Thank God! Oh, Thank God!" And then everybody turns to you to see why you're not similarly jubilant.

This brings us to the actual taking of the exam, and the second rule for passing: Do not panic!

There is no reason you should panic. You've taken hundreds of exams, and this one is different only in length (two days in most states; two and a half in California, where everyone is too laid back to hurry).

People do get unusually ner-

---

*The country's biggest supplier of these materials is Harcourt Brace Jovanovich Legal and Professional Publications, operating under the trade name "Bar/Bri." The U.S. Supreme Court recently upheld an antitrust challenge to Bar/Bri's price-fixing agreement with a (formerly) competing company in Georgia. Bar/Bri operates in thirty-nine states—how much are they charging for the course and materials in yours?

COPING WITH FEAR: CONTINUE TO WRITE!

You don't have to be a naturally timid person to experience fear during the bar exam. You could easily pick it up from somebody else.

Fear is contagious. When the person next to you begins to toss cookies, your own stomach may begin to churn. This is understandable, like the feeling you get when the pilot of your airplane begins to strap on a parachute.

Suppress this feeling. Continue to write. Whatever happens, continue to write.

If the person next to you has a heart attack, continue to write. If *you* have a heart attack, try to gut it out until the proctor calls "Time!" If you can't last that long, be sure to gasp loudly or wave your arms to catch the proctor's attention; those around you with any sense will continue to write.

---

vous, however. The physical environment is unfamiliar. The people around you are strangers. The exam proctor couldn't find your name on his list.

If you feel a wave of panic about to come over you, try to nip it in the bud. Slap yourself hard and remind yourself that you have never failed an exam in your life. If you have failed a number of exams in your life, remind yourself that no one has yet been jailed for failing the bar. (First offenders usually get a suspended sentence.)

At the end of the second day, when the final "Put down your pencils" has been called, you will feel giddy, like a marathoner crossing the finish line.* This is partly because of all the nervous energy you have expended. You may also have forgotten to eat for several days.

At this point you should do three things: First, go home and take a nap. Fatigue contributes to depression. When you wake up, you will have only the vaguest memories of the agony you have just been through.

Second, resist talking about the exam. If you still need to be told this after all these years, you are probably an incorrigi-

---

*You may also smell a bit funky. The analogy to the marathoner crossing the finish line is again apt.

PANTHEON OF LEGAL GREATS...

William Howard Taft—27th President, 10th U.S. Chief Justice. Too enthralled by the law even to take time off for exercise. Gave new meaning to "the weight of authority."

Louis D. Brandeis—famous not only as a brilliant jurist and the first Jewish Supreme Court Justice, but also as the originator of "Brandeis briefs," mammoth sociological volumes that gave new meaning to "the weight of authority."

Clarence Darrow—defense lawyer. More famous for the case he lost, the 1925 Scopes "monkey trial," than any he won. Immortal portrayal by Henry Fonda in Inherit the Wind. *No impact on term "the weight of authority."*

. . . AND NOT SO GREATS

U.S. Justice David Souter—Is this not the face of an ax murderer? You decide. Claimed to *live with his mother . . . so did Norman Bates.*

Robert (Mephistopheles) Bork —former federal judge. Nominated to Supreme Court, rejected on aesthetic grounds. When Nixon was turning over rocks in search of someone to fire Watergate investigator Archie Cox (Elliott Richardson quit rather than be the hatchet person, as did the next-in-line), guess who crawled out?

Edwin Meese III—former U.S. Attorney General. Recipient of 1st Annual "John Mitchell Ethical Standards Award." Shown here responding to press inquiries as to the continuing viability of the Bill of Rights.

ble jerk. View this as one last chance to redeem yourself.

Third, take as much vacation as you can possibly afford. Once you start work, you may not have a similar opportunity for decades.

You will not get the results of the exam for three or four months. The inherent horribleness of this delay will be exacerbated by rumors about lost exam booklets, unprecedented failure rates, and cheating scandals that will require everyone to take the exam again. Ignore these. The same ones surface every year—apparently by spontaneous generation, although Creationists decry this secular view.

The important thing to remember is that eventually you will pass. If not the first time, the second. Or the third. Just ask John Kennedy, Jr.

What you really need to worry about is what comes after that.

CHAPTER SIX

JUDICIAL CLERKSHIPS

Why Wait Until You're Fifty to Play God?

⚖

Top law students often spend a year or two after graduation working as assistants, or "clerks," to judges. This label is unfortunate. When you tell lay people you're "clerking," they say, "Don't worry. I'm sure you'll be able to get a job with a private firm sooner or later."

Lay people don't understand. The primary virtue of clerking is that it enables you to begin work with a private firm later, rather than sooner.

Whether clerking is a great deal or merely a good deal de-

The Courthouse on the Island of Tobago—the ultimate clerkship.

pends on three things: the type of court, the judge, and the location.

The Location

Starting with the last first, the location is important for the obvious reason that it's more fun to spend a year in San Francisco or New York than Utah or Alaska—unless you're a Mormon or a walrus (and even some walruses don't love Utah).

The Judge

As for the judge, if she's brilliant, her clerks may learn something. If she has Cheez-Whiz for brains, the educational value of the experience may be less.

Even more important than her intellect, however, are her temperament and work habits. Regarding temperament, you need to watch out for the not inconsiderable number of judges who are unstable or just plain mean—either because they've always been that way or because they've been on the bench so long (and thus been boot-licked by local lawyers for so long) that they've lost all sense of personal restraint. You can't believe how some very prominent judges routinely scream at and otherwise abuse their clerks.

Then there's the matter of work habits. Judges don't *need* to be workaholics; most aren't. They don't *have* to do anything that strikes them as unappealing; few do. But some judges come into the office at dawn. They're in every weekend. They drive their clerks crazy.

These judges are to be avoided, unless you're talking about one who is truly top notch, or well connected up at the Supreme Court, or both. If you're going to work that hard, you might as well be at a private firm and get paid for it.

The Court

There are two questions a prospective clerk should ask about the type of court:

1. Is it a state court or federal court?

The best that can be said about clerking for a state court judge is that it beats unemployment, depending on the welfare allowances where you live. Actually, Oliver Wendell Holmes was on the Massachusetts Supreme Court, and the California Supreme Court has had several members whose names can still be found in the casebooks (for their *good* rulings). Still, local judges are usually on a par with local politicians—which says it all.

The federal courts are a dif-

The U.S. Supreme Court, where the finest legal minds in the country gather—to serve as clerks to the Justices.

ferent story—except for the Tax Court, the Court of Claims, and a few others that no one quite knows what they do.

A federal clerkship at any level offers decent pay, plenty of prestige, and considerable educational value. Unless the judge is stupid, mean, and located in Buffalo,* you can't go too far wrong.

2. Is it a high court or lower court?

THE SUPREME COURT

Clerking on the Supreme Court is *the* legal credential, guaranteeing a faculty position at any school, or a drone position at any firm. Moreover, it's fun. Here you enjoy not only warm collegiality, but plush marble chambers, state-of-the-art word processing equipment, and a

*This geographic reference in an earlier version of this book prompted complaints from federal judicial chambers in Buffalo, New York (from a clerk suffering frostbite of the cerebrum). I wish to make clear that this slur is not *necessarily* directed at Buffalo, *New York,* but *might*

be directed at any of the fifteen localities in this country named Buffalo (located in fourteen states; South Dakota has two). No doubt most of these places are entirely worthy of the fine animal after which they are named.

basketball court on the top floor —the highest court in the land.

A slight qualification: Although clerking on the Supreme Court is fun, it's that way only for the first eighty hours of work per week; by then it's Thursday, when you'd normally be gearing up for the weekend.

Those who speak most often of the workload are the clerks to Justice Stevens (because there are only two) and those to Justice Blackmun (because there are only four). But this is somewhat like billionaires complaining of difficulties in servicing their yachts. No sober person

WHAT DO JUDICIAL CLERKS DO?

All judicial clerks do pretty much the same thing, namely, whatever their judges tell them to do. Some judges make their clerks pick up their laundry, sharpen their pencils, and help them don their robes. Some even require menial chores.

Clerks spend most of their time, however, doing three things: First, they deal with the mountains of paper that come in. Those $50,000 briefs that large law firms consider suitable for framing—clerks use them to soak up spilled coffee.

Second, clerks research the cases cited in the papers to make sure the lawyers aren't stretching the truth—or, more accurately, to gauge the extent to which the lawyers are stretching the truth.* This is a critical function, for obvious reasons.

Third, clerks write the final rulings, or "opinions," that go out under the judge's signature. The level of input from the judge varies depending on a number of factors, including the clerk's talent, the judge's talent, and—most important —the judge's comparative estimation of the two.

Some question the desirability of allowing brand-new law grads to write the opinions that make up the common law of the nation, but in general it's probably a good thing: Clerks get to be clerks because they're bright and work hard; judges get to be judges because they know somebody.

*Sometimes clerks play a more substantive role. See The New York Times, D-2 (March 8, 1983): "Where do judges get their economics?" said Philip Areeda, a Harvard Law School antitrust law professor. "From their clerks."

turns down a clerkship with the Supremes.

THE DISTRICT COURT

The District Court level is great, too. Here you see trials, confessions, and sentencings—which you savor with the bloodlust of plebeians at the Colosseum.

Moreover, you deal with lawyers on a daily basis. Litigators who wouldn't return a call from the president come running out of the bathroom to catch calls from clerks. Beware letting this go to your head, however, or life will be a lot harder for you next year, when the same law firm partners who are now sucking up to you will exact their retribution in spades.

THE CIRCUIT COURT

The Circuit Court has the least going for it in terms of giving you a new experience. Compared to a District Court clerkship, it has two advantages: a somewhat better shot at a position in academia, and a much better shot at a clerkship with the Supremes.

As a Circuit Court clerk, your only contact with the outside world comes once a month when your judge joins two other Circuit Court judges to hear oral arguments, with one lawyer saying the District Court made a mistake and the other lawyer saying it didn't.

You won't hear witnesses testify as to how the fight broke out. You won't see the tears of the spurned lover on the stand. You won't feel the hot rage of the convict screaming, "Prison bars can never hold me!" as they drag him away.

Clerking on the Circuit Court is as much like Law Review as a job can be.

CHAPTER SEVEN

RECRUITING

"I Got All Dressed Up Just to Talk to This Yutz?"

⚖

Recruiting has much in common with fraternity rush. Both involve forced smiles, frequent handshakes, too much to drink, questions that no one cares about the answers to, and a general lack of dignity.

Recruiting is important, however. Let's face it: Getting a job is what it's all about. Not many people go to law school because they can't think of anything else to do with all their money.

Law firms come in all shapes and sizes. Baker & MacKenzie, the McDonald's of law firms, employs well over a thousand lawyers in its numerous offices around the world. Solo practitioner Larry "Was that a siren?" Durkin employs a part-time secretary in Lubbock.

Some firms specialize in a single area of the law, such as communications (usually in Washington, D.C.), securities (usually in New York), or toxic sludge (usually in New Jersey).

Regardless of what kind of firm you want to work for, you need to know how to handle yourself on the recruiting circuit.

The primary rule to keep in mind about recruiting is that law firms, like lemmings, have no independent sense of judgment. They want you if they think their competitors want you. They're less interested in your credentials than in how their competitors view your credentials. Thus, your basic goal is to make them think other leading firms have already made you an offer or are on the verge of doing so.

"Nice guys, but an odd firm. They practice the law of the jungle."

This doesn't mean you have to lie to anyone. You can achieve the desired effect simply by dropping the names of other big firms in town—what you think about Cravath's associate-rotation program, how O'Melveny's new offices struck you, why you're not sure if Covington is right for someone in your particular situation.

If anyone asks if these firms have actually made you an offer, you can usually say that you haven't heard from them yet—which is particularly true if you've never interviewed with them.

Interviewing

In order to get a job at a law firm, you usually have to survive two stages of interviews: the on-campus screening and the full-scale assault at the firm's offices. Each of these stages calls for different strategies and techniques.

THE ON-CAMPUS INTERVIEW

The on-campus interview lasts twenty to thirty minutes. If your résumé shows you're at the bottom of your class, there's nothing you can do in that brief a period to get a "callback" short of stroking the interviewer's upper thigh or offering her a $2,000 hit of the leading export commodity of Bogota. Conversely, if your résumé lists you as the Law Review editor-in-chief, you'll be hard put to *avoid* getting a callback, even if you show up in a sweaty T-shirt and a Sinead O'Connor haircut.

Most applicants fall somewhere between these extremes. If you're a member of this bland majority, it is essential that you master the fine points of the on-campus interview.

This interview is too short for you to figure out what substantive qualities the interviewer thinks are important and then persuade her you're chock full of these qualities. You have to score your big points on personal style.

This means more than wearing matching socks, having your fly zipped, and remembering the name of the firm in which you're supposedly eager to spend the rest of your professional career.

It means being distinctive, memorable. It means not boring the hell out of the interviewer with weak questions that you should already know the answer to ("How big is your firm?") or that the interviewer can't possibly care about ("Would I have my own office?"). It means asking questions not about her firm, but about her personally ("Did you have any expectations when starting at the firm that weren't met?"), so she'll have an opening to talk about the subject that most interests her, namely, herself. The applicant who does this is consistently remembered as "a stimulating, thoughtful conversationalist."

Prep yourself on the firm in advance (your library will have all sorts of data on file), so you can dazzle the interviewer with the incisiveness of your questions. If you can find out in advance who the interviewer will be, prep yourself on *her* (the background of every lawyer at every firm is in your library's *Martindale-Hubbell* directory), and drop complimentary references to her college, her hometown, the year she was born.

Be diplomatic with this "informed" approach: The interviewer won't enjoy talking about the recent SEC censure of her senior partner, nor will she care to speculate on her brother's chances of parole.

Finally, if you have any choice in the matter, schedule your-

Interviews are no time to be shy. Law firms appreciate aggressiveness in their associates.

self for one of the first interviews in the morning, when the interviewer is still fresh and doesn't feel like she's going to throw up if she sees one more eager beaver in a new suit who really has no idea of what he's getting into.

THE OFFICE CALLBACK

The most important thing to remember about the office callback is to go easy on the coffee and tea. Every person you meet will offer you some, and you cannot win the "battle of the bladder."

Otherwise your strategy should be pure Dale *"How to Win Friends and Influence People"* Carne-gie: Talk about whatever your interviewers find most interesting. For lawyers this means talking about themselves.

It isn't hard to get them going. Ask them what kind of

If all else fails, what's a little begging when your career is at stake?

law they practice, how long they've been at it, what got them into it. Lawyers love contemplating their origins and destinies.

Toward the end of an interview with a partner, throw in a question or two about the firm and its practice, just to let him know you're a serious worker. You'll strike a particularly responsive chord if you inject references to "billings" or "profits" —anything related to money.

With an associate, you're as well off not asking about the firm at all. The associate has probably just turned away from ten or twelve legal documents with pages numbering in the triple figures, and the last thing he wants to talk about in this hiatus is more law.

At some point in your interview with an associate, express your curiosity as to whether partners are able to recognize the talents of their star associates (including, by clear implication, the one you're talking to). Every associate feels underappreciated, and this comment will render you instantly likable in his eyes.

If you ever find yourself short on conversation topics, take note of the trappings of your interviewer's office. The things he has on display are things he likes to talk about, things he's proud of. If he has an oar hanging on his wall, ask him if by chance he crewed a boat in college. (Be sure to say "crewed," or perhaps "rowed," but never "rowed crew." People who rowed —morons who never heard of sails or propellers—are very particular about the terminology.)

If he has a picture of himself and a former president on the wall, ask how he got to know George or Ron or Jimmy.

You're probably best off *not* attempting to compliment an old geezer on the lovely picture of his granddaughter—it could turn out to be his fourth wife.

THE RECRUITING LUNCH

A standard part of the recruiting ritual is an expensive lunch. When you're an indigent student, this can be a major occasion, both as the first square meal you've had in weeks and as your first taste of legal largesse.

If you're in the right frame of mind, a recruiting lunch can be a lot of fun. Your escorts will usually be associates, rather than partners, and they may take full advantage of the outing to enjoy themselves and run up an enormous bill that they can charge to the firm.

A recruiting lunch can also be a prime opportunity to get the real scoop on the firm, de-

RECRUITING-LUNCH DISASTERS

No matter how relaxed a recruiting lunch may seem, don't let down your guard. You're constantly on trial. Avoid any form of gaucherie, regardless of how many rounds of applause it may have drawn in your fraternity or sorority dining room. And beware these common mistakes:

1. At a Chinese restaurant, don't blow your nose on the bread pancake that comes with the moo shu pork.
2. At an Italian restaurant, never order spaghetti or anything else likely to get friendly with the front of your shirt.
3. Wherever you are, don't touch the hard rolls. They always fall apart and generate a pile of crumbs as big as a basketball.
4. At any nice restaurant, resist the urge to pop one of those round, yellow, tasty-looking mint-like things in your mouth, because it is probably a butterball. If you do make this mistake, do not attempt to ameliorate the situation by declaring, "Now *that's* a good butterball."
5. If the bill passes within your visual range, do not let out a long, low whistle and exclaim, "Hot *damn,* I didn't know we broke a window!"
6. If a little dish of water arrives at the end of the meal, don't drink it.

pending on how many drinks the associates have and whether they're the sort who feed on one another's gripes: "You think *you* got shafted by that partner, listen to what the son of a bitch did to *me* two days ago. . . ." Encourage them to continue in this vein.

If they offer you a drink, do you accept? Sure—*you* don't have to go back to work. This is especially true if your hosts order something; you don't want to be a stick in the mud.

What to order? This is not the time to play "stump the bartender." Go with wine—it's classier than your usual rum and coke. And don't look surprised when the waiter asks, "Red or white?" Wine *always* comes in colors—but not beige, teal, or seersucker.

Above all, do not feel guilty about the cost of the meal. It's not *your* fault they're trying so hard to impress you. Just view this as part of your reward for accumulating a good record. Besides, whatever firm you go with will take it out of you soon enough.

The Résumé

Do not waste your time producing a flashy résumé. Lawyers don't know enough to appreciate good packaging and would view a really slick-looking résumé with skepticism, even scorn. Lawyers just aren't into glitz; they're into drab—which they think shows them to be people of substance, rather than form.

What they're really interested in is your grades. They *might* consider outside activities that show an unusual ability to stomach huge piles of grunt work. This does not include being a Red Cross blood donor or a bag boy at the local supermarket. It *does* include being a proofreader at the Sanskrit Publishing Center or shoveling stable strudel at a fertilizer plant—*these* say something about your suitability for private practice.

If your grades are good, put them front and center. That's easy. The tougher question is,

what if they're terrible? What if the only A you ever got was in one of those touchy-feely, get-your-head-together social-relations seminars in which everyone got A's because the bearded instructor/guru from California didn't like to pass negative value judgments?

That's a tough one. Interviewers aren't just passing time when they ask about your grades. If yours are truly awful, you have two options. One is to look him in the eye and assert with cool confidence, "These marks don't reflect what I can do"—and hope they buy it. (Be sure to say *"these* marks" rather than *"my* marks"—the goal is to dissociate yourself from them, as if they were somebody else's.)

Your other option is to look him in the eye and assert with cool confidence, "My name is Dan Quayle, my daddy is rich, and he'll make it worth your while to hire me." History suggests this is the more effective approach.

Note two items *not* to include in your résumé. First, in describing a previous summer clerkship (if you've done one), don't bother saying "Researched and drafted memoranda and performed other litigation tasks." Lawyers know what summer clerks do—and it's not exciting enough to warrant elaboration.

Second, regardless of your grades, don't clog up the "Per-

Vice-President Dan "It's better to be lucky than smart" Quayle— living proof that grades aren't everything.

this firm because it has a varied practice that you believe would offer a stimulating as well as challenging introduction to a career in the law.

Cut to the chase. You don't need to sell them on their own firm.

If you have something to say, say it in your résumé—with a few possible exceptions, such as the fact that your entire family now lives in South Dakota, so you're serious about the prospect of moving there (a proposition otherwise hard to swallow), or that your mother speaks well of their firm, and she should know—she's their *biggest client.*

sonal" section of your résumé with "Health: Excellent." Law firms don't care about your health. Take a look at the people interviewing you, with their paunches, skinny arms, and pasty complexions. Is *their* health excellent?

The Cover Letter

All a cover letter needs to say is "Here's my résumé. Got a job?"

Okay, dress it up a little with the more formal "Enclosed is my résumé" language, but don't bother with the oft-heard stuff about how you're applying to

Recruiting Letters

Every recruiting letter has one of three basic messages: "Yes," "Maybe" or "When hell freezes over." If the letter you get carries the last of these messages, you needn't worry about what else it might say. But if it says "Maybe" or "Yes," you need to be able to read between the lines in order to know where you really stand.

To aid you in this process, set forth below are two pairs of recruiting letters. In each pair, the first letter shows what the firm actually said, the second what the firm really meant:

THE YES LETTER

What the firm *said*:

Powell, Goldstein, Goldchain & Goldwatch
1 Peachtree St., Rd., Ave., Blvd., Dr., Cir., Lane, Etc.
Atlanta, GA 30303

October 31, 1991

Mr. Louis T. Grizard
906 Johnson Hall
Columbia Law School
New York, NY 11743

Dear Mr. Grizard:

I enjoyed speaking with you at Columbia. You have an excellent record, and on behalf of the firm I would like to extend an offer of employment.

We would be pleased to have you visit our offices to meet more of our attorneys. If you are interested in pursuing this invitation, please call me or our recruitment coordinator, Ms. Lucy Bramnick, to arrange a mutually convenient time for your visit.

I look forward to seeing you again.

Sincerely,

Katherine J. Nudsen

Katherine J. Nudsen

What the firm *meant*:

Powell, Goldstein, Goldchain & Goldwatch
1 Peachtree St., Rd., Ave., Blvd., Dr., Cir., Lane, Etc.
Atlanta, GA 30303

October 31, 1991

Mr. Louis T. Grizard
906 Johnson Hall
Columbia Law School
New York, NY 11743

Dear Mr. Grizard:

For a guy from a trade school in Harlem, you make quite an impression. Your pale complexion, emaciated physique, and overall nerdiness, combined with your incredibly high grade-point average, suggest that you are precisely the sort of compulsive, library-loving grind we're looking for.

No doubt you'll have a lot of offers, because hard-core zealots like you aren't a dime a dozen. Someone so patently willing to sacrifice his health and social life is a real find.

I wouldn't want to introduce you to a client or have to eat a meal with you, but I'll bet you could rack up enough billable hours in a year to reduce your salary to the equivalent of $1.95 per hour.

I sure hope we can sign you up.

Sincerely,

Katherine J. Nudsen

Katherine J. Nudsen

THE MAYBE LETTER

What the firm *said*:

Craven, Swine & Less
43 Park Avenue
New York, NY 10014

October 31, 1991

Ms. Georgine Covington
413 Jefferson Hall
University of Virginia
Charlottesville, VA 22207

Dear Ms. Covington:

I enjoyed speaking with you when I was at "Mr. Jefferson's University" last week. Although I am not able to make you an offer of employment based on our meeting, I would like very much to have you visit our offices for further interviews.

If you are interested in pursuing this invitation, please call our recruitment coordinator, Mr. Allen Williams, to arrange a mutually convenient time for your visit. By the way, you might find it helpful to coordinate your visit with interviews at other area firms.

I look forward to seeing you again.

Sincerely,

Ms. Claudia Carter

Ms. Claudia Carter

What the firm *meant*:

Craven, Swine & Less
43 Park Avenue
New York, NY 10014

October 31, 1991

Ms. Georgine Covington
413 Jefferson Hall
University of Virginia
Charlottesville, VA 22207

Dear Ms. Covington:

I was astonished that someone like you—a mediocre student at a state university—would bother to interview with Craven, Swine & Less. Even allowing for the diminished capacity that no doubt afflicts even the strongest of minds after a few months of "living" in a pissant town like Chucklesville, I have to say you're one pitiful specimen.

On the other hand, a bald willingness to ask for something you have no right to is worth a lot in this line of work, as we made clear in a recent bankruptcy proceeding.

You couldn't possibly have a real future with us, but we always need more bodies, and we can bill your time at the same rates as our decent associates. Clients can't tell the difference.

I'm not willing to take sole responsibility for hiring you, so you'd better come up and meet a few more of our people.

By the way, unless you can sucker some other firm into picking up the tab, you'll be sleeping on a bench while you're here.

Sincerely,

Ms. Claudia Carter

Ms. Claudia Carter

Recruiting Misrepresentations

Law firm recruiters, like used car dealers, are known for their willingness to misrepresent reality. Their misrepresentations often deviate so far from reality as to constitute what lay people would call "lies."

Lies told by law firm recruiters and used car dealers are not punishable under the law. They're not even called lies; they're called "puffing." Examples of puffing by used car salesmen are: "There will always be a resale market for this Edsel" and "This Yugo couldn't be safer."

Set forth below are ten of the most common recruiting lies, each translated into what recruiters *would* say if they were burdened by a proclivity for truth:

What Recruiters *Say*

1. Our associates work hard but like it.
2. You'll get excellent training at this firm.
3. We have one of the more diversified practices in the city.
4. We believe in lean staffing of cases.
5. We don't spend the entire day at the office.
6. Our lawyers maintain a variety of outside interests.
7. This firm likes to keep a low profile.
8. We encourage *pro bono* work.
9. We believe in bringing associates along one step at a time.
10. We have a policy of carefully controlled growth.

What Recruiters *Mean*

1. Our associates work hard.
2. After three years here you'll have all the skills of a legal secretary.
3. We'll take any kind of work that comes in the door.
4. We make each associate do the work of three.
5. We take a lot of work home.
6. Three years ago we had an associate whose spouse used to play the piano.
7. Nobody has ever heard of this firm.
8. We tolerate *pro bono* work on weekends.
9. You'll be indexing deposition transcripts for years.
10. We're losing clients.

THE OPEN-DOOR POLICY
"We welcome constructive criticism from our associates."

Law firms boast of their openness to criticism and reform. They claim to observe an open-door policy with respect to associate grievances and speak of their eagerness for thoughtful suggestions from below.

Once you become an associate, try them out. Suggest keeping the office heat on during winter weekends because it's difficult for the associates to write while wearing ski mittens. Request facial quality toilet tissue, i.e., something softer than computer paper, in the associate restrooms.

The response from any partner you approach will consist of "I'm glad you mentioned that. You know, it was a problem when I was an associate. It's a problem, sure enough."

This response is intended to convey the message "I know how you feel. I've been there. I'm a regular guy."

It also conveys the message "I'm not going to do anything about it. No one is. Take it like a man."

So much for the open-door policy. Until you're a partner yourself, hang on to your ski mittens and your personal roll of White Cloud two-ply tissue.

Associate Committees

If associates have grievances, why not band together to make their views known? Why not, in other words, unionize?

The basic explanation is ambition. Associates see no long-term benefit in improving the lot of associates, because they don't plan to *be* associates ten years down the road. They plan to become part of management.

Moreover, they know partners would welcome associate organizing about as warmly as George III welcomed the Boston Tea Party—and would deal with an associates' union the same way Frank Perdue would deal with a union of oven-stuffer roasters.

UNDERSTANDING BILLABLE HOURS

When lawyers talk about billable hours, they usually refer to annual figures. Set forth below is a chart that breaks down the annual figures into weekly figures and then puts them into perspective.

In evaluating these figures, keep in mind that billable hours don't (or *shouldn't*) include time you spend eating lunch, calling all over town to get a date, or discussing last week's episode of *L.A. Law*. An accepted rule of thumb is that forty billable hours requires sixty hours at the office (except in New York, where you start billing as soon as you wake up).

Annual Total	Weekly Average (50 weeks)	Interpretation
4,000	80	Wrong profession; medical intern
3,500	70	Pathological liar
3,000	60	Barely conceivable, and then only if living with cot in office.
2,500	50	Sweatshop hours. Brutal but possible, given lots of travel. Probably guilty of substantial bill padding.
2,000	40	Very respectable figure in most cities.
1,500	30	Civilized life-style, assuming no heavy non-billable duties.
1,000	20	An associate with this number had better be working for her parents' firm.
500	10	Of counsel (in Montana).
25	.5	Deceased (but no one has realized it yet).

Hard Questions

The reason law firm recruiters don't dread interviews is that law students don't know enough (or are too timid) to ask the Hard Questions. But interviews are no time to be a jellyfish. Go into every interview prepared to ask any or all of the following Hard Questions:

1. How does the firm determine associate salaries? Are raises and bonuses based on sheer merit, or instead on "productivity" (euphemism for "hours")? If productivity, does the calculation include *pro bono* work, recruiting, client development, and other activities an associate may be "asked" to spend his weekends doing but often gets no credit for?

2. How many associates have left the firm in the past six months? The past two years?

3. What does the firm offer in the way of associate training? Is it all "on the job," i.e., nothing?

4. Are any associates working on a single big case? If so, will *you* be assigned to that sinkhole of a case?

5. How much *pro bono* work does the firm do *as a percentage of its total billable work?* (These days any place that does as much as five percent calls itself a "public interest" firm.)

6. Did most of the partners go to the same school? Do most of them attend the same church, temple, shrine, or sacrificial altar?

7. How many hours does the average associate bill each year? (This figure should be lower than the total number of hours in a year.) Does the firm announce a "budgeted" (read "required") number of billables? Most important, *what were the average billables of the last group of associates to make partner?*

8. Does the firm have any "non-equity partners," i.e., people who are held out to the world as partners but in fact get a fixed salary and are *not* tenured? ("Non-equity partnership" is a sham device for postponing the day of real partnership, perhaps indefinitely.)

9. Ask your interviewers—especially the ones you really like—if they will still be at the firm one year from now. If you get a mush-mouthed answer, ask how many headhunters or other firms are now in possession of their résumés. You can't believe how many soon-to-be-departed lawyers continue to be scheduled for recruiting interviews because they haven't yet gone public with their plans to leave.

PRACTICAL SKILLS THEY OUGHT TO TEACH IN LAW SCHOOL—*BUT DON'T*

1. Faking interest during interviews.
2. Not believing ninety percent of what they tell you when you're a summer clerk.
3. Masking your awe at the size of your first paycheck.
4. Masking your disappointment at the size of your twenty-fifth paycheck.
5. Dealing with sexual advances by senior lawyers.
6. Dealing with sexual advances by messengers.
7. Sucking up to secretaries and other support staff.
8. Pretending you don't think lay people are stupid.
9. Sleeping with your eyes open. (Hey, fish do it.)
10. Not worrying about the cost to the client.
11. Generating excuses for incredible screw-ups.
12. Mediating between your brain's craving for coffee and your bowels' craving for peace.
13. Slipping away every Tuesday for psychotherapy.
14. Pretending you don't hate everyone at your firm.
15. Pretending you don't regret going into law.

CONTINUING LEGAL EDUCATION

PRACTICAL SKILLS THEY OUGHT TO OFFER VETERAN LAWYERS—*BUT DON'T*

1. Not talking about law at social occasions.

2. Resisting the call of nature during contract negotiations.

3. Making bills look reasonable.

4. Pretending summer clerks aren't presumptuous idiots.

5. Pretending the associates who work for you may someday make partner.

6. Persuading rich people you're a fantastic lawyer.

7. Persuading indigent friends and relatives you're a crummy lawyer.

8. Sucking up to secretaries and other support staff.

9. Pretending you respect your partners.

10. Pretending you trust your partners.

11. Pretending you like your partners.

12. Pretending you like your partners' spouses.

13. Pretending you've never fooled around with your partners' spouses.

14. Reconciling the demands of work and getting divorced.

15. Slipping away every Monday—Friday for full-scale psychoanalysis.

16. Getting a life.

CHAPTER EIGHT

HOW TO SURVIVE (AND MAKE PARTNER) IN YOUR LAW FIRM

You can make it to the top if you know what to kiss, and whose.

⚖

Each day of associateship in a law firm is like walking a tightrope over shark-infested waters: One wrong step could spell doom. Most associates walk this tightrope with their eyes wide shut.

Survival is the name of the game, and in order to survive in a law firm, it is critical to keep in mind this simple fact: The partners run the show.

To be sure, some of them run more of it than others, and the idea (which they hold out to the public) that one is accepted as an equal upon attaining the status of "partner" is as accurate as saying Liechtenstein is the equal of Russia because they're both "sovereign jurisdictions," or that a '65 Impala is the equivalent of a Sherman tank just because they get the same gas mileage.

The main point from your perspective, however, is that partners are tenured (sort of) —and you're not. It is hard to get rid of one of them—and easy to get rid of you. Therefore your goal must be the cultivation of their approval.

Over time this cultivation may

"Remember, Cogswell: Associates are fungible, partners are not."

become odious. As one associate commented, "They should make my senior partner Pope. That way all I'd have to kiss is his ring."

Assuming you can stomach the thought of prolonged obsequiousness, how can you ensure that the partners will vote thumbs-up when your name comes up for partnership eight or nine years down the road?

There are two reasons any partner might vote to invite you into the club: (1) He likes you, or (2) he thinks you'll make him rich.

Practically speaking, he may like you *because* he thinks you'll make him rich—a not uncommon confluence of motivations. Just recall that great, warm-nosed dog you had as a child, which nuzzled up to you and wagged its tail when it saw you coming—as long as you continued to feed it.

Try to think of the partners as large, furry Labradors with unusually strong appetites.

In order to make the partners like you, you need to make them think you're *like* them, that you're one of them. You even want them to think of you as a surrogate son or daughter, unlike their actual sons and daughters, who snort cocaine, wear their hair in spikes and play in rock bands with all the talent of Milli Vanilli. Also, in order to make the partners think you'll make them rich, you need to convince them you're the hardest-working, least likely to screw up, most anal, puritanical grind since Cotton Mather.

To succeed in this dual quest, there are a number of specific rules that must be followed. These are key maxims that you would be well advised to tape to your bathroom mirror for review every morning as you tie your tie or trim your nose hairs.

Strict adherence to these rules could gain you a window office, with a secretary who will type one-page letters and deliver phone messages within several days of when they come in. Deviation from them could land you in an interior office across from the messengers' washroom, sharing a surly secretary whose idea of good service is not popping gum too loudly while listening in on your private calls.

Rule 1.
Cover Your Ass.

This rule is the most important of all the rules, as well as the most difficult to adhere to. The reason it is difficult to adhere to is that its command embraces everything you do, no matter how trivial. A discussion of all the applications of this rule could fill several volumes, but for present purposes some examples will have to suffice:

1. Supervise everything your secretary sends out in the mail. The stories are legion of the wrong letter going out in the right envelope, or vice versa. If your secretary mixes up the memo you intended for your client, in which you observe that his gold bullion sales in Switzerland "might" have consequences for his income tax obligations, with the letter you intended for the IRS, saying your client has nothing else to report, you might as well start cleaning out your desk.
2. Proofread everything—carefully. This is all the more true when a partner hands you a document and says, "Take a quick look at this and then send it out." He might very well think it's fine when he gives it to you, but . . . why is he giving it to you?

   What you're seeing is an instinctive effort to cover *his* ass. If a legal argument proves to have been stated inaccurately, or the numbers just don't add up, you can be certain that the next document you proofread will be your résumé. Remember: When a partner and an associate are working together, the associate is deemed responsible for the screw-ups of both.

3. Before sending out any brief, memo, or other document, clear it with someone—anyone —senior to you. The point is to place the responsibility for screw-ups anywhere but on yourself. Not only should you run any document past a senior person, but (a) dictate a "memo to file" that you've done so, and (b) somehow let an *even more senior* person know you've cleared the document with the person in-between.

4. Notify and consult the client regarding everything you do on his case or project. Clients don't affect you directly, but they can always complain to the partners, and in rare instances they will even get hot enough about something to sue the firm. Your aim should be to build a record— consisting of letters to the client covering *everything*— to put the client in the position of appearing responsible for anything that screws up (which can happen for reasons totally beyond your control).

Partners, you will find, are the ultimate ass coverers in this fashion, spending enormous amounts of billable time drafting letters explaining to the client why the firm is doing what it is doing. This could all be done by telephone for one-tenth the expense, but such a common-sense approach would reduce billings and—even more unacceptable—leave the firm's collective ass uncovered.

5. In reporting meetings or conferences on your time sheets, never just say, "Attended meeting with general counsel of client—2 hours." If a partner was there, she may have recorded the meeting on her time sheets as lasting only 1-½ hours. Even if you were the only lawyer present, the client may at some point mention to the partner that he thought the meeting lasted 1-½ hours. In either case, the discrepancy could prove disastrous. You'll never have an opportunity to prove you were the only sober, non-hallucinating, non-schizophrenic person there.

Always say *"Prepared for and* attended meeting with general counsel of client—2 hours." Those three extra words, which cost you nothing, could make all the difference.

The same principle applies when you've spent all day proofreading hundreds of

PUT THE BURDEN ON THE CLIENT

When writing a client to request that he sign an affidavit or "verify" a pleading, don't be too proud to include some weasely (yet lawyerly) lines such as the following:

> Please read, review, examine, and consider all aspects of this item carefully, thoroughly, and thoughtfully. Needless to say, you are perfectly, totally, and absolutely free to make any additions, alterations, modifications, corrections, amendments, clarifications, enhancements, breast augmentations, editions, or even changes that you feel are appropriate, necessary, desirable, worthwhile, or good. Thereafter, and only thereafter, if it meets with your full and complete satisfaction, agreement, approval, and liking, sign it and . . .

When you include this sort of material, the *client* is responsible for whatever you've produced, and your ass is covered. (For God's sake, keep a copy of your correspondence.)

pages of industrial-bond documents. It's not that you did anything wrong; you were *supposed* to spend all day proofreading those things. But dress it up a little. Instead of saying, "Proofreading —9 hours," say, "*Reviewing, editing and* proofreading—9 hours." Again, three little words could make a world of difference.

6. Before beginning work on any assignment, make sure you understand exactly what the partner wants. This is not as easy as it may sound.

The partner might want an argumentative piece that contains no reference to authority running against the client's position. He might want a general survey of the law, including all authority pro and con. He might initially want the latter, but having read your memo, decide he wants the former, and wonder why you didn't give him something he could use.

Rarely will he *tell* you what he wants. You have to figure it out.

This raises the question of what your immediate response should be with respect to a partner who has not made clear what he wants. Sometimes a partner will present you with an assignment so garbled you will suspect his sobriety.

As a rational person you will be tempted to ask questions. You will feel an impulse to attempt to clarify the problem and make sure you understand what is desired.

Resist this impulse! One or two questions are okay, three at most, just to let the partner know you're awake and paying attention as he drones on (stifle yawns at all costs).

But no more! Further inquiry, however reasonable, will only make him nervous regarding your intelligence and legal acumen. If he hasn't made the problem clear the first time around, it's probably because he doesn't understand it himself.

Your best approach, even in the face of the most wildly confused assignment, is to smile, nod your head, and murmur, "Yes," "I see," "I understand." When he has finished (as far as you can tell), you should leave the office, find a quiet place to vomit, and then track down a senior associate to tell you what the hell is going on.

7. Save all your drafts. It doesn't matter whether you're writing a $10 million oil lease, a $5,000 opinion letter, or a crummy memo to file. If you run it past a partner (and you should), and he makes

you do it over ten or twelve times (and he will), save every version. There's at least a fifty-fifty chance the partner will call you three days later and say, "By the way, Kyle, you did save those early drafts, didn't you?"

This makes no sense. If you asked the partner why he wanted them, he would say you never know when some of the material from those early drafts might prove useful. But the real reason is that he's scared—not of anything in particular; just scared, like a kid at night who calls his father to shine the flashlight under the bed.

By all means resist pointing out to the partner the absurdity of his request. Humor him. Tell him you've saved every scrap, and they're all just waiting for the time when they might be needed. And make sure they are: You never know when he'll show up with a flashlight to check under the bed.

8. Make four times as many copies of every document as you can possibly use. This is particularly true with respect to litigation briefs, for which you will need:

• an original and three copies (for actual filing);

• another copy that the court clerk will "file stamp"

and return to you so you can prove to the partners that you actually filed it;

• "service copies," i.e., copies for you to serve upon (or deliver to) all opposing lawyers;

• intra-office copies (send one to every lawyer who had anything at all to do with producing the brief, and one to the partner who brought in the client);

• client copies (send copies to everyone at the client's offices you ever talked to or heard might have an interest in the case);

• your own copy;

• fifteen copies for people you have never heard of, but who will materialize out of the woodwork as soon as you have filed the things, asking for copies that they will never read;

• ten copies to replace the other copies that will turn out to have missing pages or that your secretary will have used to clean gum off the bottom of his shoe;

• ten copies just to have around, so you can truthfully answer in the affirmative when a partner asks if you made some extra copies in case of an emergency.

This last point is particularly true. If you do not make a ridiculous number of extra copies, the partner in charge will find out and be irritated that you did not make a ridiculous number of extra copies.

Also, and most often overlooked, you should get the client to sign *several* copies of everything you may need to file that requires the client's signature. The concern is that if the original is lost, someone will have to crawl to the client for a second signing. This is crazy, of course, and savvy clients who

*Make extra copies of everything!
It could save your legal career.*

recognize ass covering for what it is will be irritated. There is a better than even chance, however, that some partner will ask if you had the good sense to take this precaution, and you will need the tangible proof at hand.

Rule 2. *Take on as Few Work Assignments as Possible.*

This rule may seem inconsistent with what you've heard about the brutal hours associates are required to work, but it isn't. I'm not saying you shouldn't generate some impressive hours, and I'm definitely not saying you shouldn't *appear* to be working extremely hard. (*See* Rule 4.)

I *am* saying that your goal should be to do a *great* job on a *few* projects, rather than a *so-so* job on *lots* of projects. Mediocre reviews can be fatal in this highly competitive field, no matter how early in your career they slip into your file.

Don't worry about having a small number of reviews, if they're good. Leonardo da Vinci completed only seven paintings; Snickenberger did hundreds.

Why would anyone give you a mediocre review, you may justly wonder, if you're doing decent work while carrying a heroic workload? Why wouldn't the partners take the sheer volume of your work into account, and how could they expect the usual level of perfection from an associate who is doing the work of four?

In this regard it is critical to note three points about how law firms work. First, partners are no less selfish than anyone else on the street, and they are extremely attuned to covering their individual asses. (*See* Rule 1.)

They don't care about your work for anyone else. Each one will expect perfection from you on *his* assignment, and if he doesn't get perfection, he will (a) resent it, and (b) remember it.

Second, almost never does one partner in a law firm have any idea of what demands another partner may be making upon you. They operate in black boxes, isolated from each other (and often the world). It is fatal to assume that partners communicate with each other and that they will not make conflicting demands on your time. They don't, and they will.

Third, it is a verity that partners have short memories with respect to associates' contributions to the firm as a whole. Your overall performance may have been superlative in view

REIGNING IN THE PARTNER

A critical skill every associate needs to develop is that of preventing the partner with whom you're working from saying something foolish or just plain wrong in front of a client.

Partners tend to bluff a lot in client meetings, and sometimes one of them goes too far. Maybe he doesn't know the terrain, or maybe he's just feeling good and gets carried away. Whatever, he starts giving advice that you know could send the client into bankruptcy or prison.

Your job in this situation is to stop him.

Doing so requires alertness, because you have to see very quickly where the partner is going and cut him off before he reaches the point of no return.

It also requires diplomacy, because you have to intervene without exceeding too far the limits of your humble station. (You're only there because the partner likes an audience or might want coffee.)

One approach is to interrupt him in mid-sentence:

"Mr. Hanifen, I can see you're about to present another of your typically brilliant ideas, but perhaps we should first explain to Ms. Claire the more conventional approach, so she'll know what her competitors are doing."

If the outrageous proposal is already on the table, you could say:

"Another way to achieve the same objective—you were explaining this to me just yesterday, Mr. Hanifen—would be to . . ."

Either of these displays of uncommon boldness on your part will probably startle the partner, like a bucket of ice water, into recognizing what he was about to do. At that point he will follow up with:

"Huh? Oh, yes. Yes, absolutely. We could do that, too. Options, Ms. Claire—we want you to know all the options."

The partner won't love you for this, because he'll feel foolish about it. He definitely won't thank you for covering his ass.

But don't let the certainty of his ingratitude prevent you from helping him out.

Remember: Whenever a partner looks foolish, an associate's head rolls.

of the number of balls you were juggling at one time, but you can be certain that a few years or even a few months down the road, anyone who may once have known the full story will have long since forgotten it.

Undoubtedly your spartan sacrifices will win you points in the eyes of the Deity. But when partnership evaluation time rolls around, those baggy-eyed months when you foreswore sex and averaged three hours of sleep per night will mysteriously disappear from the collective partnership memory.

This problem of conflicting demands made on associates is hardly of recent vintage. Indeed,

having heard of it repeatedly over the years from involuntarily departing associates, partners at most firms are prepared with two facile responses of which you should be aware.

First, they say, associates are expected to act as "professionals," i.e., to do top-quality work on *everything* they undertake. As a practical matter, this is utterly unresponsive to the problem of conflicting demands on associates' time. Nevertheless, partners continue to hoist the ill-defined, self-promoting, semi-macho banner of professionalism with respect to a number of irrational expectations.

The second reply partners

"Let's not concern ourselves with partnership, son. A man's reach should exceed his grasp, or what's a heaven for?"

make with respect to conflicting demands is that associates should be mature enough to protect themselves. In this regard, take them at their word: C.Y.A. Make sure your butt is covered but good.

This is easier said than done. The safest and most frequently available approach is to pit the partners against each other, relying on their varying levels of seniority to resolve the problem. Thus, when all your available time is being used on a project for Senior Partner Wescoe, and Junior Partner Goetz approaches you for help, your response should be no less obsequious and yet self-protecting than the following:

GOETZ: Son, I'd like you to help me draft a prospectus for an offering of convertible debentures that the local power authority plans to offer next week.

YOU: That certainly sounds interesting. I enjoy drafting prospectuses and have long been fascinated by the interface of federal securities laws and local power regulation. May I assume you have already spoken with Mr. Wescoe, who said he wanted my full attention devoted to his mother-in-law's will for the next two months?

GOETZ: Wescoe, eh? Let me get back in touch with you. I

think maybe I can find someone else.

YOU: Please let me know if there is any way I can help. I had no plans for this Saturday evening that couldn't be rescheduled for next year.

Note that the only people you can interplead in this manner are partners. Law firms aren't like poker, in which two deuces are better than one ace. In law, one partner tops four associates.

Rule 3. *There Is No Such Thing as a "Draft."*

In legal circles, some words and expressions have become altered through usage. They take on peculiar meanings, remote from popular understanding. They become what are known in the law as "terms of art."

One important term of art is the word "draft." Failure to understand its specialized meaning has left many an eager and capable associate consigned to proofreading loan agreements for the (short) duration of his stay with the firm.

The potential disaster of misunderstanding the term draft will confront you early in your career: A partner for whom you've been researching an issue asks you to provide her with a "draft" of a memorandum or brief on that point. More often than not she'll camouflage the trap by saying something like "Just get me a *quick* draft," or "Just *whip off* a draft," or even "Just *dictate* a *rough* draft." The emphasized words should trigger flashing red lights in your mind.

The partner who utters these words does not mean them. When she speaks them, she should be disbelieved. There is no correlation between her expression and her intent.

Notwithstanding how your dictionary might define "draft" ("a first or preliminary writing, subject to revision"), and notwithstanding all your understanding of the language acquired through a major in English, a minor in Linguistics, seven years of Latin, three of Greek, and over two decades of actually using words in spoken and written communications, this partner wants *a polished, final product!*

That she asked for a draft does not mean she will tolerate typos. That she directed you to produce a "rough" working document does not mean you should not have double-checked all your citations in advance. That she said "dictate" this piece does not mean she will excuse the absence of captions, headings, and subheadings.

Everything you submit to a partner should be suitable for framing. No matter how casual the request, how insignificant the task, or how few the dollars at issue, the test you should apply to everything bearing your name is its suitability for hanging in the Sistine Chapel (the *newly restored* Sistine Chapel) of legal documents.

Note an ironic corollary to the rule that there is no such thing as a draft: Everything is a draft.

The point here is while everything you submit to a partner should constitute your best possible effort, you should never *admit* that it constitutes your best possible effort. This is because the partner will want to change it—not because it necessarily needs changing, but because changing things is what partners do.

For this reason you should type at the top of everything you submit to a partner, especially things that are ultimately headed for a client or judge, the word "Draft." This conveys two important messages: first, that this is just a preliminary product, something you could undoubtedly improve upon given a bit more time; second, that *of course* the partner's *invaluable* input will be necessary to put the document in truly final form.

The first message covers your ass, the second sucks up to the partner—two entirely appropriate messages for someone in your position to be sending.

The communication problem exemplified by partners' consistent misuse of the word "draft" occurs in a variety of contexts. Two other notable examples: "Just skim the cases," and "Take a quick look at the cases in this area."

Never should an associate "skim" anything, and never should an associate take just a "quick look" at anything. If you miss one case that is even colorably relevant, or one statute just arguably germane, it will haunt you five years down the road.

A last word regarding drafts and other preliminary undertakings: If, in the direst of circumstances, you find yourself unable to complete the exhaustive, perfect work you now know is expected, do not forget Rule 1: C.Y.A.

The best way to do this is to state the limits of your work in a memorandum accompanying your product. In such a cover memo, do not hesitate to say,

> In the following discussion, I have, as requested, addressed the question of liability under Securities and Exchange Commission Rule 10b-5. *I have not addressed the question of damages in connection with such liability.*

The emphasized second sentence, although spineless, serves to shift the burden higher up for any catastrophic problems that occur. It suggests, without saying so, that there was an *understanding* that you would limit your research as stated.

OTHER MISLEADING EXPRESSIONS

When a partner misuses the word draft, you can protect yourself—*if* you've read this book and know what she really means. Lots of times, however, a partner will say something that signals danger, but there's nothing you can do about it—nothing, that is, short of throwing up on her desk to cut her off before the ax falls.

In some instances this will prove to have been a moderate response.

Set forth below are several serious danger signals that associates should recognize for what they are.

1. *"This project will require some creative thinking."* The partner who approaches you with these words is cunning. He is about to present you with a problem that he knows has no solution.

   Sometimes a client wants to do something she can't do—such as pave over Lake Tahoe to build a parking lot. Sometimes a client *doesn't* want to do something the law says she *has* to do—such as (if she's Washington, D.C.'s delegate to Congress) pay her taxes.

Whatever the problem, the partner will come to you for a solution.

This is one of the more craven things a partner will do. He *knows* there's no solution, because he's thought about it and couldn't come up with one—which is what led him to the remark about creative thinking.

Even if you could come up with a solution, he wouldn't use it, because there's no authority for it. If there were any authority, he'd know.

This partner is covering his ass. He'd rather you be the one who failed to come up with a solution, in case he has to explain it to an even more senior partner or to the partner who brought in the client.

If he *is* the partner who brought in the client, or the senior-most partner of the firm, he's covering his ass anyway, out of sheer instinct. After all, that's what got him where he is.

2. *"Have you ever done any work on _____?"* (Insert "Arkansas contract law," "condo-conversion restrictions" or "FCC cellular-communications regulations.")

The partner who asks this question does not care about the answer. If your answer is no, she will say, "Fine, you're about to get into the area." If your answer is yes, she will say, "Fine, we're going to take advantage of your expertise."

Her question is rhetorical. It is an indirect way of saying you're about to tackle the most god-awful area of law known to man. She is justifiably squeamish about presenting the assignment head-on.

3. *"Are you busy?"*

Your answer to this question should always be "Very busy."

Whoever asks this question is planning to give you an assignment, probably a bad one or he wouldn't have approached you obliquely with the question. (If he approaches you with the even more oblique query, "How are you fixed for time?" you can be sure the assignment has four legs and barks.)

If your answer is merely "Busy," you will get the assignment. You may get it even with "Very busy," but that way you'll at least gain points for carrying a heavy load.

If in fact you're not busy and you think you need the hours, your answer should

LOATHESOME CLIENTS—
DO YOU HAVE
TO TAKE THE ASSIGNMENT?

Occasionally you will be asked to help represent someone you don't like. It's not just that the work is tedious and boring (that's to be expected), but that you find the client repugnant for ideological or other reasons. Do you have to take the assignment?

It depends. Are we talking about your average, garden-variety thug—Manuel Noriega, say, or Marion Barry? If so, the answer is yes, you definitely have to take the assignment. That's what big firms do. Those kinds of clients are their bread and butter.

But what if it's someone really awful, someone so unspeakably vile, loathesome, and hideous that you lose your lunch at the mere thought of the person—George Steinbrenner, say, or Leona Helmsley? Do you still have to take the assignment?

No. But you don't have to remain employed at your firm, either. Turning down an assignment is risky business.

Actually, sometimes you can get out of bad projects. But moral reasons won't do it. Tell the partner that you're already busy helping some *other* odious, repulsive slug stay out of jail. Say, "Gee, I'd love to help you get John Gotti back on the street, but I've got all I can do keeping Charles Keating free to pillage the public coffers."

Whatever you say, don't attempt to explain your true views to the partner in charge of the gruesome work. He knows people scorn him for what he does, and he's hypersensitive to criticism. This is simply no place for candor.

There's a lot of ugly work floating around at the top firms, because the clients who can afford them didn't get that rich by being nice folks. If you don't like wearing a black hat, you should consider a different job.

be the same, but with a qualifier (preferably couched in language suggestive of your heroic capacity for toil): "Very busy, but perhaps I could *shoulder* some more."

4. *"This is just a one-day project."*

This lie ranks up there with "The check is in the mail," "It's only a cold sore," and "Partnership is guaranteed."*

There is no such thing as a one-day project, at least not one they'd bother calling in a new person to work on.

"One-day projects" usually involve searches for a case or rule that does not exist. Most likely the people in charge have already checked the obvious sources and found nothing. Because your search will turn up nothing, too, you will be required to continue it for days on end, wasting incredible amounts of time as you descend the ladder of obscure sources.

5. *"Familiarize yourself with the law in this area."*

The partner who says this is setting you up for a fall. He doesn't mean you should merely find out which title of the U.S. Code contains the statute he's referring to. He doesn't mean you should become just roughly conversant with the structure of the legislation in question. He's using "familiarize" in the way only partners use it: to *master* an area; to commit to memory every case and every clause in every statute.

It may be that he's just got wind of a fast-breaking deal, or he anticipates a dramatic turn of events in a big case. Whatever, he thinks it'll happen fast, or he wouldn't have given you even the little warning that he did. Moreover, he thinks the area is too complicated to be responsible for it himself. He wants someone else's neck on the line: yours.

Rule 4. *Cultivate the Image of a Workhorse.*

In law, appearance is reality.

This rule mandates affirmative craftiness and cunning. It exhorts you to be resourceful and creative in your quest for the proper image.

To assist you in this quest, set forth below are some lifesaving (and marriage-saving) tips on how to maintain the preferred image while keeping your work load under control. These tips fall into five categories:

---

*No letters, please—we know the one about oral sex. Everybody does. But this is a PG-rated parody.

"A little advice, son. Practice the courage of your convictions outside the office."

SETTING YOUR WORK LOAD: THE PROPER MEASURE

Let's start with a fundamental fact: *Billings are important for your career.* Even at the firms that advertise themselves as laid back and "full of individuals who value their lives outside the law,"* the partners' greatest lament is that there are only twenty-four hours in an associate's day.

*What these firms are "full of" is something quite different, and much better for plant growth.

The fact is that in a law firm, some level of work is unavoidable. But *what* level?

The answer to this question depends on your peers at the firm: For appearance's sake, you're going to have to spend roughly as much time working as they do.

But only *roughly* as much. This brings us to one of the major tips I can offer to ease your burden: Do not so much as *think* about trying to lead your class in billable hours.

Not even if it's a class of two.

For one thing, you won't be able to do it. There are always a few superhuman grinds around.

More important, that's not how you want to spend your life. You want more on your tombstone than "G. Mackay Smith, Partner." You'd like at least enough spare time to be able to show up for your divorce.*

The only goal you should set for yourself in this area is to avoid the anchor position in your class. That's good enough. For once in your life, as contrary as it is to your nature, be average.

EASY HOURS: HOW TO BEEF UP YOUR BILLINGS LEGITIMATELY

Given that you're going to have to chalk up some hours, you should take every possible advantage of the few easy but legitimate ways of beefing up your billings.

Most of your work will not be easy. It will consist of something like researching U.S. postal regulations, drafting motions for enlargement of time (only a lawyer would attempt to "enlarge" time), or comparing the Delaware non-profit-corporation statute to that of the other states, Puerto Rico, Guam, and Louisiana.

Such work is boring (you will find yourself filling out time sheets for fun) and tedious (the mental equivalent of needle-point). It is comparable to digging ditches in a mine field, which doesn't take much intelligence, and isn't glamorous or enjoyable, but you have to pay very close attention to what you're doing.

When something easy comes your way, pounce on it. Of the various easy but legitimate ways of beefing up your billables, at least three will be available no matter where you work.

Travel

The first—and best—of these is travel. A shrewd associate will involve himself in work for Sri Lankan or New Caledonian clients, preferably corporate work that could entail trips to company headquarters. The time spent en route to these places is billable, and it is a piece of cake from your point of view. Sure, you *might* have to spend the travel time reviewing client papers—or you *might* have to order a double Jack Daniels and watch *Rocky 9* on the airplane movie.

Defending Depositions

The second source of easy hours involves defending depositions. This means accompanying your

---

*Under federal law, anyone who goes without sex for two years can be declared a statutory virgin.

client to respond to some other lawyer's demand that your client answer questions about a lawsuit. All *you* have to do is sit still and listen.

To make your client feel secure (you're there in a sort of hand-holding capacity) and to prevent yourself from falling asleep, you should object periodically to the line of questioning, whatever it is (you're also there in a sort of justice-obstructing capacity).

This means challenging it on grounds of "form" (how it's worded) or "relevance" (what it has to do with anything).

If the client is a key witness in a big-money case, it's a good idea to pay attention. You'll never encounter that situation as an associate, however, so don't worry about it now.

Proofreading

Finally, there are easy hours to be had in proofreading. Every writing that leaves the firm has to be proofread. The partners expect it to be done, and the clients expect, however grudgingly, to pay for it.

You don't want to find yourself proofreading too often: It's boring, and it looks silly on your résumé as your primary field of expertise. Still, proofreading has the prime virtue that frequently

---

GETTING AWAY FROM IT ALL

Projects that get you out of the office are not to be taken for granted. Better yet are projects that not only get you out of the office, but get you someplace where it doesn't matter how you're dressed.

Even if this means going to a law school library to perform a fifty-state survey of local franchise laws, or to a client's warehouse to rummage through boxes of ancient records, you will come to relish any opportunity to shed those suit pants (which never fit quite right anyway), that absurd tie (whose only function is to collect tangible memories of your meals), or those accursed pantyhose (which only make it hard to go to the bathroom).

Note: If you're wearing the absurd tie *and* the accursed pantyhose, being stuck in the office isn't your primary problem.

NON-BILLABLE WORK

Non-billable work (also known as "administrative" time) consists of such activities as recruiting, running the summer program, doing *pro bono* work, and writing articles and speeches (that partners will take credit for).

The basic question regarding non-billable work is: Do partners appreciate it?

The basic answer is: Not much.

At best, these things won't significantly *harm* your chances for partnership.

This is particularly true with respect to *pro bono* work. Regardless of what they may have told you when you were interviewing, partners view *pro bono* work as a form of private charity. Their attitude is: "We don't care if you want to do it, but do it on your own time."

The same is true for speeches and articles. Most of these won't even bear your name, and the few partners who once knew you were the author won't remember it three months later.

As for being appointed to run the summer program, most associates view this not only as an honor heralding a glorious future with the firm, but also as a daily opportunity for a free lunch.

"Maybe I'm getting too old. I can remember when we did
pro bono *work for nothing."*

There is no such thing as a free lunch. While you're playing camp counselor, your peers are meeting clients and developing expertise. *They're* becoming lawyers.

What about the honor of being appointed to such a high-profile position? Don't be naive. Either your substantive work is more dispensable than anyone else's, or you're such a grind that the partners know you'll eat the time—that is, you'll run the program during the day and keep up your billables at night and on Sundays (on Saturdays you'd be working anyway).

Don't let anyone give you the runaround about how such work builds "goodwill" and "appreciation" around the firm. Half the partners think summer clerks should be treated with kid gloves, and half think they should be made to earn their keep. Thus, no matter how you run the program, half will think you screwed up.

Besides, when partners really appreciate something, they reward it with *cash*. In this regard your motto should be, "Let others have the goodwill. Give me the dough."

you can arrange to do it *at home*, stretched out on your sofa in your underwear eating Doritos and listening to Vivaldi or Merle Haggard. Also, catching a few typos that everyone else has missed (a "catch" in legal parlance—as in "Nice catch, Otis. I didn't see that one") can earn big points in the eyes of the partner overseeing the project.

WEEKEND WORK: AVOIDING IT, SIMULATING IT

A legal career inevitably involves weekend work. It was a lawyer who said, "Thank God it's Friday —only two more workdays until Monday."

A question confronting all associates is how to know when weekend work is really necessary. Legal work is like schoolwork, in that you could always do more in a given area. (Or like psychoanalysis, in that the more you get into it, the uglier things look.)

Your goal, of course, is to minimize weekend work. Free weekends are what it's all about.

To keep your Saturdays and Sundays as carefree as possible, keep in mind that weekend work is of two types. First, there is serious, big-time work that has been brewing for a long time. It could be a major antitrust suit that you've been involved in, the papers are due on Monday, and you are, by any standard, the logical person to spend the necessary weekend time buffing up the brief.

There is no escape from such work. You should resign yourself to it, exploiting the opportunities it will afford to enhance your image as a hard worker. If the partner in charge takes the extraordinary step of *asking* whether you will be able to help out over the weekend, and you have sized up the situation and see that you are clearly the logical choice for the job, tell her you're definitely in.

Moreover, pretend you're glad about it. Tell her you were already planning to be there. Tell her you *like* weekends at the office, because they give you a chance to hunker down without lots of interruptions from the secretaries. (Do not worry about your credibility in this regard: Lots of partners really do like weekends for that very reason.)

Above all, do not make her order you to be there. She'll do it, so you won't have gained anything, but she won't like doing it. Once you've started rubbing her conscience the wrong way or convinced her that you're not a team player, you

might as well ease on down the road.

The other type of weekend work is emergency work: short-term, last-minute, run-of-the-mill stuff that any associate could do. This type of work you can avoid.

This isn't *your* emergency; it isn't something they need *you* to handle. It might be that a judge has just asked some partner to brief an issue by Monday, or the local prosecutor has just summoned a client to appear before a grand jury.

More likely, some partner hasn't bothered taking care of a matter that has been around for a long time, because he knew there was a full stable of associates he could get to handle it at the last minute.

Any associate can handle these types of emergencies, and you shouldn't be concerned about the propriety of trying to avoid them. What you should be concerned about is *how* to avoid them. It can be done. (*See* "Friday Afternoons," below.)

You might well wonder about the costs of such an approach. Won't people get angry if you consistently manage to avoid weekend work? Most likely no one will know. No one keeps a list of weekends worked. Still, it's worth covering your ass here, as everywhere. There are three especially handy devices for doing this.

FRIDAY AFTERNOONS—
THE ART OF LAYING LOW

Friday afternoon is a critical time. That's when partners start checking their calendars to see what's on tap for Monday. That's when your weekend stands its greatest chance of being destroyed.

Try to avoid answering your phone over these hours. Definitely do not check with your secretary or receptionist for messages. (Once either of these has told you some partner is looking for you, you're caught. After the way you've treated them, no support staffer can be trusted to hide the fact that you don't return calls on Friday afternoons.)

Avoid walking past partners' offices on the way to the bathroom. If possible, don't even *go* to the bathroom over these hours. If you absolutely have to, consider finding a nice stall and staying there the entire afternoon.

Ideally you should arrange to be out of the office altogether; an appointment with your chiropractor will do. If that isn't possible, the next best strategy is to set up camp in an obscure corner of the library. Just take your books and papers and whatever you're working on with you. Don't worry about how it looks; lots of people keep mountains of garbage there.

Be sure it's an *obscure* corner of the library. Not infrequently a partner needing bodies will actually prowl through the library in search of hapless associates for weekend duty.

Also, you want to be able to ignore your name when it goes out over the paging system; if you're in a crowded area some jerk will tap you on the shoulder to say he thinks he just heard your name.

What about matters you actually need to handle over these hours? Use the library phone to call your date regarding weekend plans. Everything else can wait till Monday.

*"Too busy? Oh, no sir, I'm not too busy. My desire
to Shepardize knows no bounds."*

First, many firms have a receptionist come in for all or part of each Saturday. This affords you a great opportunity. Whether you are at home, at the beach, or at a friend's place on Saturday morning engaged in some horizontal recreation, set the alarm for about eleven, call the office, and (using a false voice) have yourself paged.

Everyone who is really at the office will assume you are there, too, somewhere. That they haven't seen you won't matter: Law firms are big places. And don't worry that the receptionist will know you haven't answered your page; lots of people don't answer pages.

Why eleven? Most people who work on Saturday do so in the morning, so if you call later you might miss them, as well as the receptionist.

On the other hand, the really senior people who come in generally won't do so *before* eleven, so you don't want to call too early.

Besides, it *is* the weekend.

Another handy device for simulating weekend work is more effective but also more demanding. It involves actually going in.

This doesn't have to ruin your picnic plans. You don't have to *stay* there. Just go in, look a bit fatigued (not *too* fatigued; you're supposed to be able to take the pressure), walk briskly through the library, grab two or three reference volumes, return to your office, turn on the light, and then head for the links.

Turning on your lights is important. The cleaning personnel will have turned off all office lights on Friday evening, so anyone who sees your light burning on Saturday thinks you've been in.

The joy of this trick is that it keeps working all weekend. In many office buildings the cleaning staff won't be around again until Monday night, so you get the benefit through Saturday evening, all day Sunday, and even Monday at dawn.

Turning your light on after the cleaning people have passed is a trick capable of application during the week in many firms. If the cleaners make their rounds past your office around seven most evenings, and you happen to finish your squash game at the gym next door at seven-thirty, stop by and turn on your light. It can't hurt your image with the partners who pass by later that night or the few who come in early the next day.

As long as you're in on any weekend, consider leaving some kind of note on the desk of a partner, just to let her know you were in. You have to be careful with this device, because it can be a bit transparent. Don't do it *every* weekend, and don't write in red ink at the top of the note "Saturday, 7:00 P.M." Let the partner figure out when the note must have been written, as by observing that it was written on the back of that weekend's church bulletin.

The third method of simulating weekend work requires you to ingratiate yourself with the guard stationed at your office building on weekends. With flattery and a bottle of scotch, you may be able to persuade him to sign your name on the check-in list that office buildings maintain on Saturdays and Sundays.

All those who actually come by will see your name as they sign their own names. Better yet, they *won't* see a mark beside your name in the check-*out* column—clear evidence that you've outlasted them all.

The only danger with this trick is that others may be doing the same thing. If fifteen associates' names appear in alphabetical order in identical script, someone may sense a sham.

ALL-NIGHTERS

All-night work has much in common with weekend work:

It's unpleasant and should be minimized, but it gives you an excellent opportunity to enhance your image as a hard worker.

Like death, all-nighters cannot be avoided indefinitely. When your number comes up, remember two points: (a) Do it gracefully, and (b) don't keep it a secret.

The first point is of primary importance. Because everyone has to pull an all-nighter at some time, no one is going to

"Dudley here just pulled his first all-nighter. Brings back some great memories, doesn't it?"

The All-Nighter. Prolonged sleep deprivation can produce anxiety and insecurity in even the sturdiest associate.

feel sorry for you. If you bitch about it, you won't even get credit for your dedication, because everyone will know you did it involuntarily.

The preferred posture is one of ease and nonchalance. This suggests that you are possessed of unusual stamina. (Let your colleagues think you wouldn't *ever* go to bed but for social reasons.)

It also suggests that you do this sort of thing all the time, which carries the further implication that other, more senior lawyers view you as the

person to call upon in a crunch—the can-do guy. Over time it will have partners and associates alike believing that you get called in for the *hard* cases.

The only problem is that your Hemingway-esque grace under pressure will be wasted if no one knows about it. Hence the second point: Don't keep your all-nighter a secret.

In practice, this point can conflict with the goal of handling the all-nighter gracefully. Talking about it is inconsistent with shrugging it off as commonplace. Thus you should make considerable efforts not to pull your all-nighters alone. With someone else present, word of your energy and stamina will spread.

If you cannot finagle company for the duration, do not despair. You can make your exertions known to the partner in charge of the project by showing up in his office the next day wearing the same clothes you were wearing the day before.

When doing this, make sure your clothes are orderly (shirt tucked in, belt buckled, brassiere facing forward), because you don't want to look out of control. However, your shirt should be suitably wrinkled, and your beard shadow suitably dark (particularly impressive on women)—these things you can't be expected to do anything about.

Another reason you should not be too distressed by the absence of company for your all-nighter is that when you're alone you can take naps on the conference room sofa. Before lying down on that sofa, however, take the precaution of arranging for a trusted friend (preferably someone outside the firm) to ring the conference room telephone early the next morning. It's professionally embarrassing to be caught blowing big-league Z's when you're supposed to be polishing up a brief.

GENERAL IMAGE TIPS

Keep your secretary busy.

This is especially important if you share a secretary with a partner. The partner will gauge your productivity from your secretary's pace.

If you are sharing a secretary with a partner, none of your work will get done. The secretary will use the partner's work as a pretext to avoid yours so she can finish the latest issue of *Cosmopolitan*. She isn't there to *work* eight hours a day—at least not for some lowlife associate.

Nevertheless, you must make the effort.

One way to give the impression of keeping your secretary busy is to keep her in-box loaded with papers. What kind of papers doesn't matter. If you need one letter copied, attach that letter to two or three large files and leave the whole stack in her box. The partner will see the stack and be impressed.

Another way to generate a large volume of material for your secretary's in-box is to use a separate cassette for each letter or memo you dictate. With one hour's labor on Monday morning, you can produce enough tapes to suggest a whole weekend of work.

Some particularly important image tips relate to those occa-

Signs of Life

1. *Light burning brightly. (Tape the switch in the "on" position, so the clean-up crew won't flip it off once you're gone.)*
2. *Coat on the back of chair.*
3. *Uncapped pen.*
4. *Full cup of coffee. (Make sure it's full; half cups are common.)*
5. *Smoking cigarette. (Check your local novelty store for those Perma-lite cigarettes that give off smoke for hours.)*
6. *Half-eaten sandwich. (How long could you last on a half-empty stomach?)*
7. *Phone with blinking "Hold" button. (Dial your home phone, which will ring until you get in from your night on the town, and punch the "Hold" button and leave.)*
8. *Open Federal Reporter.*
9. *Shoes. (How far could you get without your shoes?)*
10. *Open briefcase. (Keep a second one around for this purpose. You should be carrying your first one with you when you leave.)*
11. *Open drawer. (Partners are too fastidious to believe you'd leave it that way all night.)*
12. *Legal pad with writing cut off in mid-paragraph, or even mid-sen . . .*

sions when you need to go home a little early—say, around lunchtime.

This will occur once in a while. Hey, you have a life. But cover your ass.

You can do this in several ways. First, always leave by the stairwell rather than the elevator. Even if you're on the fortieth floor. A partner who sees you boarding the down elevator will be suspicious, no matter how full your briefcase or purposeful your stride. (By all means carry a briefcase, not your squash racquet.)

Next, prepare for the calls that might come in after you've gone. You don't want partners being told you went home after half of a workday (or one fourth of a workday in New York).

Tell your secretary or receptionist, whoever will get your calls in your absence, that you're off to a meeting (you don't need to say *which* meeting). Say you'll be back when it's over, but it might not end until after the office closes. The point you want to convey is that although she might not see you again until tomorrow, she should tell callers that you've gone "out," not "home."

If you're worried that a partner who gets this message might work late that night and wonder why he didn't see you around, call in for messages after nine holes. Otherwise, just be pre-

pared to say that because of where the meeting was held, it was more efficient to stay there to finish reviewing "the papers" (there are always papers) than to return to the office.

What about partners who stop by your office and see no signs of life? Make sure there *are* signs of life.

Your light should be on, of course. That's basic.

But go the extra mile. Leave a suit coat in plain view, on the back of your chair or the arm of your sofa. Shrewd associates keep an extra coat constantly on hand for this purpose. (Be sure you leave a suit *coat*, not suit *pants*. The implications are entirely different.)

Also, leave a full cup of coffee on your desk. Lawyers make a lot of money, but they just can't believe someone would waste a full cup of coffee.

In your quest for the image of a workhorse, keep in mind that you can score big points by being in the right place at the right time. If your firm's administrative committee or other ruling body meets over coffee and doughnuts every Thursday at 7:30 A.M., find some excuse for strolling by their conference room every Thursday at 7:30 A.M.—with your sleeves already rolled up and your hair *not* still wet from your morning shower.

The same principle applies on

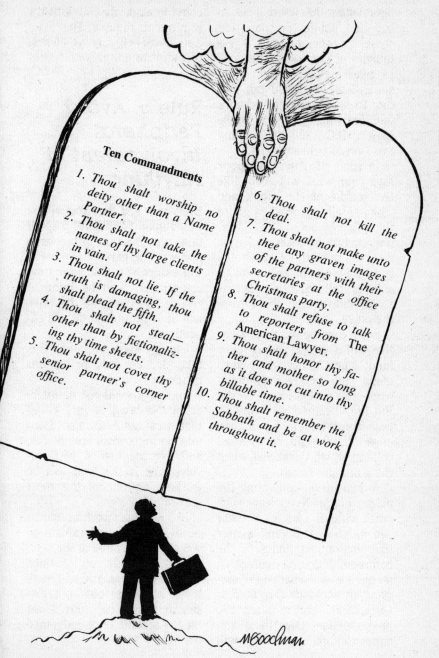

Ten Commandments

1. Thou shalt worship no deity other than a Name Partner.
2. Thou shalt not take the names of thy large clients in vain.
3. Thou shalt not lie. If the truth is damaging, thou shalt plead the fifth.
4. Thou shalt not steal— other than by fictionalizing thy time sheets.
5. Thou shalt not covet thy senior partner's corner office.
6. Thou shalt not kill the deal.
7. Thou shalt not make unto thee any graven images of the partners with their secretaries at the office Christmas party.
8. Thou shalt refuse to talk to reporters from The American Lawyer.
9. Thou shalt honor thy father and mother so long as it does not cut into thy billable time.
10. Thou shalt remember the Sabbath and be at work throughout it.

NBoodman

days when the weather is so bad that public transportation ceases to operate, and three-fourths of the secretaries call in swearing their cars won't start. Sometimes you can predict these disasters in advance (such as when you're in Washington, D.C., and the evening news predicts heavy dew).

In such situations, set your alarm for what will seem like the middle of the night, and make an all-out effort to get to the office by seven. Invariably, one or two partners will have done the same thing, motivated by white-collar machismo to be able to tell their friends the storm didn't keep them from the office.

When they see you there early, they will recognize you as "their kind of guy." They won't commend you—you're only doing what you're expected to do. But they'll remember it and always think better of you than of your lightweight, candy-assed colleagues, who weakened when the going got tough.

A final tip on cultivating the proper image: Never leave your office without a book or yellow pad in hand. It doesn't matter that you're just going to the bathroom. It doesn't matter that no one can see what you're carrying (it could be *Our Bodies, Ourselves*). You're after the proper *image*. Over the years, subconsciously, partners will come to associate you with the implements of labor. That association will help carry you where you want to go.

Rule 5. *Avoid Peripheral Involvement in Anything.*

Every now and then you will be called upon to perform a small task in connection with a large project. The partner in charge will assure you that your time commitment will be minimal and that your end of the work will be both interesting and educational.

Use any excuse to avoid this task. It can only bring you misery.

Your work will not be interesting. No case is so interesting that it cannot be broken down into boring constituent pieces, and the premise of your involvement is that you will be working on one of the most subordinate pieces.

Nor will your work be educational. No one will explain to you the background of the case, or bother to keep you informed as to its progress. You will work in an absolute void—not dissimilar from what your social life has become since you joined the firm.

"He read my memo. Then he told me ignorance of the law was no excuse."

That the work will be boring and educationally worthless is the least of your problems. *Lots* of your work will be boring and educationally worthless.

The main problem is the enor-mous potential for damage to your reputation. Once you have done anything on a case, peo-ple expect you to know every-thing there is to know about it, and they think you an incompetent imbecile if you don't have every one of its details at your fingertips.

They forget the limited nature of your involvement and become irritated by your lack of comprehension. The fact that you don't know what is going on is not rendered forgivable in their eyes by the fact that no one has *told* you what is going on.

To add insult to injury, you are forever after on call for emergencies requiring weekend work and all-nighters in connection with the case. In big cases, emergencies occur all the time, and an associate who has done as little as fifteen minutes of work on such a case is considered to have special responsibilities with respect to its most onerous tasks.

This problem of peripheral involvement in a large case is not unlike that of becoming marginally familiar with an objectionable area of the law. Once you have so much as glimpsed the Federal Submerged Lands Act or stubbed your toe on the U.S. Code volume containing the Federal Insecticide, Pesticide and Rodenticide Extermination Act, you are forever after deemed the firm's expert on those subjects. Buying a stamp at the post office qualifies you as your firm's expert on U.S. postal regulations.

The lesson? Scope out all projects in advance. Where possible, avoid those that strike you as odious, regardless of how minor your involvement is promised to be.

Remember: Your willingness to play the role of the courteous dinner guest, cheerfully consuming whatever slop is put before you, will only bring you second, third, and fourth helpings of the same.

Rule 6. *Give the Partners Something Practical.*

If you want to succeed as an associate, shed all pretensions of scholarship. Practicing law is a trade. Notwithstanding what you learned in law school, a lawyer is like a garage mechanic, except that the lawyer charges more because his lunch pail is made of leather and called a "briefcase."

Lawyers like to think of themselves as scholars. It's how they explain to themselves why they don't earn as much as investment bankers.

Nevertheless, what partners want out of you when they ask for a memorandum is something they can insert wholesale into a brief or send directly to the client.

This doesn't mean your prod-

uct should be clear and readable. You *are* a lawyer.

But it should not be a Law
Review article. If you produce a
think-piece or an academic treatise, they'll make you do it
again.

No doubt this will frustrate
you. Throughout law school the
professors emphasized the schol-
arly aspects of law. You learned
that writing for your school's
Law Review and reaching impossible conclusions was where
it's at.

Ignore all that. Satisfying
clients is what the partners are
trying to do. Satisfying partners
is what you're trying to do.

Rule 7. *Stay Alert to Your Long-Term Prospects.*

If you are content at your firm
and doing well, there is no reason you should not stick around
indefinitely. On the other hand,
if you are going to leave your
firm, whether voluntarily or on
a rail, you should know that a
junior associate enjoys greater
mobility with respect to other
firms than a senior associate.

This is partly a result of inter-
firm competition and pride. The
top firms are hypersensitive to
the suggestion that they might
be willing to take on an associate who didn't cut the mustard
elsewhere. Some of the best cre-
dentialed firms are the most insecure in this regard, snubbing
"used" associates with a disdain
more appropriate for used den-
tal floss.

Also, law firms prefer legal
virgins, so to speak. They feel
that a lawyer who has spent
much time elsewhere has lost
something vital.

Finally, a young associate has
greater credibility than a senior
one in claiming that the first
firm just didn't live up to its
advertising—that it didn't, for
example, have enough work to
keep people busy past eight or
nine o'clock at night ("and I
just couldn't stay at a place
where they work part-time").

Law firm recruiters will tell
you, of course, that you'll never
have a second shot at their firm.
"Pass us up now," they'll say,
shaking their heads grimly, "and
that's it." In reality, the doors
to the church are always open.

Okay, maybe not *always* open,
or not at *every* church. And
you might have to give up a
year or two of seniority in the
transition. But you're definitely
not trapped for life.

Remember: It's a lot easier
to switch firms than to switch
spouses—and people do both all
the time.

Now, if the problem at a given
firm is that *you* don't like *it*,
you need be only marginally

BATHROOM ETIQUETTE

Partners don't like seeing associates in the bathroom. This is partly because it means the associates aren't in their offices where the partners can find them, but also because partners like having the place to themselves.

Never follow a partner into the bathroom. If you go in and see a partner already there, turn and leave. What if you're already there when a partner comes in? This depends on what you mean by "already there." If you're in one of the stalls, wait until he has entered a stall and, as far as you can tell, committed himself to being there. Then make your escape.

If you're at a stand-up urinal, simply close up shop and exit. This is no great hardship; lots of associates can't function with a partner nearby anyway. (If the partner doubles up with you at the same urinal, even though there are empty ones nearby, you face an entirely different set of issues.)

As any veteran of big-firm life can tell you, entering a bathroom at the office causes you to be paged. Entering with a newspaper or magazine triggers a minimum of forty-five calls within the next four minutes.

The toilet seats at most firms are equipped with heat-activated sensing devices that cause the paging of any individual situated thereon. Partners at the major firms would neither confirm nor deny that each associate's buttocks are individually coded into the system.

If you're determined to carry reading material into the bathroom, make it a letter or something else that will fit into your pocket. Do not stop at the reception area, stick the office copy of the *Wall Street Journal* under your arm, and head in. So brazen a declaration of your plans for the next fifteen minutes is tacky.

The combination of stress, coffee, fast food, and legal documents gives the average male the natural-gas output of Montana. Releasing this in your office mysteriously summons your secretary. Unlike your fraternity brothers, your secretary will not think this situation hilarious. Neither will you when your work stops getting done.

"What do you think you're doing, Saunders? Just killing time?"

concerned as to how *it* regards *you.* To be sure, you don't want to screw up anything so badly that they padlock your office and give several Dobermans a whiff of your handkerchief. But basically you can just walk whenever you're ready.

If, on the other hand, you are not unhappy where you are and could imagine yourself still there five or ten years down the road, you need to keep a sharp lookout for indicia of your progress vis-à-vis your peers.

There is really only one indicium, although it travels under many names: bread, scratch,

DIPPING YOUR PEN
IN THE COMPANY INKWELL

The colloquial rendering of the traditional taboo on intra-office dating—"Don't dip your pen in the company inkwell"—has been expressed in other ways as well. Most notable is the "hamburger rule," which advises against getting your meat at the same place you get your bread.

Every firm has at least one lecherous senior partner. More often than not, this person is male. Lecherous female senior partners are not common features of the legal landscape—the profession is not so advanced.

This lecher may or may not be single. He may or may not be attractive. He is, invariably, smooth and confident. He will sit down in your office, cross his legs, and straighten his tie in a slick way that says here, at last, is a guy who really knows how to sit down, cross his legs, and straighten his tie.

It may occur to you that a liaison with this person will advance your career. Don't be naive. For each lover/partner who *may* become an ally in your fight for advancement, you'll acquire forty enemies among your fellow associates, who will have a thousand opportunities to torpedo you along the already perilous passage to partnership.

Even if your ally is a big gun in the firm, his clout will not be enough at partnership time to offset the hostility of the other partners. They will scorn you for what they perceive as an obvious ploy. They will be jealous that one of their colleagues is having more fun than they are.

With respect to "horizontal integration," i.e., associates dating other associates, the dangers are less. Your motives are not suspect, because the alliance does not enhance your competitive position.

The major problem with dating another associate is, of course, what happens after you break up. Unless your firm is gigantic, you will still see each other every day in the library. You will have to suffer in silence as he or she shows up at the Christmas formal with a new date. (Groin kicks are considered unprofessional outside of Texas.)

On the other hand, who applies cost-benefit analysis to

affairs of the heart? You date who you know*—and who do lawyers know† but other lawyers at their firms? The reality is that law firms are rife with intra-office dating, most definitely including those idiotic places that try to legislate against it.

The bottom line: Sex among colleagues is a venerable tradition in the law, and you might as well get in on it before it goes away.

*Okay, *"whom* you know"—but doesn't that sound ridiculous?
†Okay, *"whom* do lawyers know"—but don't you feel silly about being so compulsive for two footnotes in a row?

jack, dough, clams, flaps, whipout, moolah, cabbage, simoleons —some have been heard to call it "money."

You will hear stories of other indicia, such as interesting work, sexy travel, nice office space, or a secretary willing to correct typos. The firms themselves will even tell you to heed your evaluations, which most of them provide annually or semi-annually and which no associate in his right mind trusts, except in negative circumstances (such as when the evaluator demands your office key and asks where you would like them to forward your mail).

But if money isn't everything, it is definitely way ahead of whatever is in second place. If you fall behind the pack in salary (or even fail to stay up with the leaders in a large class), you would be well advised to start buffing up your résumé.

ON NOT MAKING PARTNER

Even with the aid of this book, there's a chance you won't make partner. Most associates don't.

Times are hard for law firms these days, and partners are looking for reasons *not* to let you on board, rather than the reverse.

Make no mistake: Doing great work is no guarantee of partnership. Often the partners just don't feel like dividing the pie any further. And why should they? *Lots* of associates do great work. The legal profession is blessed—and cursed—with a surplus of talent.

Partnership decisions are said to reflect the Screwee Rule: They'll do it to you if they can. The only associates they can't afford to screw are those who've either developed their own clients—Young Rainmakers —or shrewdly carved out indispensable areas of expertise.

If you get shot down, ask yourself if life would have been so great if you'd made it. Are those really the people with whom you wanted to spend the rest of your life?

Not making partner could be compared to getting bounced from a leper colony: The world outside may be better than the one you're leaving.

"Every firm needs someone like you, Stokes. Unfortunately for you, our firm already has that someone."

THE STAR SYSTEM

Law firms operate on a star system. Within two or three years after starting work, a few associates are singled out from each class as the stars of that class. There's no formal awards ceremony, but everyone knows who they are.

Being marked as a star is a self-fulfilling prophecy. Stars receive the best work (such as it is) and the most responsibility —in short, the greatest opportunities to shine.

You don't get to be a star by caring about the outside world. If you've already been designated a star, you aren't reading this book.

The big question is, what if you're not one of the stars of your class? Do you bail out? Work three times as hard? Sabotage the stars?

If you're sure that being a star is what you want (and to make partner you have to be a star), hang in there for a year or two. The fact that you're not a star yet doesn't mean all the slots are permanently filled. Circumstances can cause a star's luster to fade. A star can become a black hole.

Otherwise, resign yourself to second-class citizenship and go about your business. Your salary will continue to come in.

More important, you'll acquire a certain peace of mind. Once you know you're not going to make partner, you can quit *worrying* about not making partner. You can loosen your collar, take time to read the morning paper, and schedule something for Saturday night. You can treat your work at the firm as a "job," rather than as a "career"—the difference is about one hundred hours per month.

IF YOU DON'T MAKE PARTNER . . .

What, specifically, happens if you don't make partner? You die—usually in poverty, always in disgrace. Most spurned associates go in a matter of weeks, but you might be among those who last several months—long enough to see your spouse com-

SIGNALS THAT YOU'RE ON YOUR WAY OUT

How can you tell when things aren't going well for you at a firm, that the partners consider you a short-timer, that you're on your way out?

The subtlest of the bad tidings is bad work: Your assignments, instead of growing less boring and tedious over time, continue to extend the known frontiers of boredom and tedium.

To be sure, all associate work is fairly boring and tedious, so it can be hard to discern a trend one way or the other. (It's like asking, are foreign movies more boring at the beginning or the end? Sometimes it's just impossible to say.)

A somewhat clearer sign is the "freeze-out": Assignments stop coming in at all. At first the freeze-out seems like a blessing—you're thrilled to have your evenings free, and you revel in being able to get together with friends for lunch. Then you realize your learning curve is plummeting, and you find yourself hating to go into the office because of the whispers you suspect accompany your every step.

Take heart. No longer must you sit in doubt, agonizing over whether the ax is about to fall. Set forth below are ten indicators to watch for, clear signals that you're on the way out:

1. Your new office has no desk or window, and the seat flushes.
2. The firm librarian requires you to put up collateral each time you take out a book.
3. A partner posts your latest memo on the bulletin board near the water cooler to give everyone a laugh.
4. Your annual salary raise is in the four figures— *including* the two on the right of the decimal point.
5. The firm holds its summer outing at the Scarsdale Country Club, but your invitation says "Larry's Mini-Golf and Garage."
6. Your secretary is replaced by a typewriter and a copy of *Yudkowitz's Guide to Résumés*.
7. The firm considers you for partnership every three

months, just so they can tell you you've been passed over *again*.

8. You find yourself receiving assignments from people junior to yourself—including messengers.

9. At Christmas, instead of a bonus, you get a set of luggage.

10. Your client contact is confined to trusts and estates clients whose wills have become effective.

"Then it's agreed. There is no place here for someone who marches to the beat of a different drummer."

plete the divorce proceedings and your kids change their last name.

The most common cause of death among passed-over associates is starvation, although a surprising percentage are able to transcend the immobilizing effects of depression sufficiently to take their own lives.

A few find positions as baggage handlers at airports (small, regional airports), but they, too, invariably lose their will to live once the other baggage handlers find out what happened and begin mocking them.

In any event, death seems merciful after a few weeks of the indignities that befall passed-over associates. Some of the least of these indignities are:

1. Cabbies play tricks on you, like stopping twenty yards down the road, waiting for you to run up, and then screeching away.
2. Your children come home

TEN WAYS TO END A LEGAL CAREER

1. When a senior partner in your firm announces that his wife is pregnant, distribute a memo denying responsibility.
2. After a brief has been filed, tell the partner in charge that it's too bad the baseball game you went to over the weekend was a doubleheader, because you would have liked to citecheck the cases.
3. At the office Christmas party, get drunk and barf on a partner's date.
4. Come in to the office at the crack of noon—two days in a row.
5. While defending a client in a deposition, tell him he has to answer the other lawyer's questions truthfully.
6. Explain to a client how the time he's being billed for was really spent.
7. Score with a secretary that a senior partner has been putting the moves on for months.
8. Go for a jog one afternoon and then hang your jock strap or brassiere (or both) on a conference room doorknob to dry.
9. Fail to read this book.
10. Write this book.

from school every day with bruises and bloody noses, from fights with other children chanting "Billy's father didn't make *paaaartnerrr.*"

3. Your children *stop* coming home from school with bruises and bloody noses, because they've begun denying you're their real parent and claiming they were adopted.

4. Strange dogs approach you and pee on your leg.

5. Strange people approach you and pee on your leg.

6. You pee on your own leg.

7. People bring their dogs from all over the city to walk them in your yard.

8. Guys in white sheets with pointy heads come by at night and burn a large *P* in front of your house.

9. Stockbrokers and insurance salesmen gather under your bedroom window at night and practice their sales pitches over loudspeakers.

10. Your bank sends you a notice saying you're overdrawn, and when you call to say that can't possibly be right, they say, "So sue us. You'll be dead soon. Ha, ha."

"Do you hear me? I was partnership material."

CHAPTER NINE

ONCE YOU'RE A PARTNER

The Crock at the End of the Rainbow

⚖

Your legal career could be viewed as a kind of journey —but to what?

Questioning the destination of the journey may be pointless if you're convinced you've already arrived, but for those of you who feel you're still en route, who dare to hope for something more, maybe it's not too late.

The mere thought of partnership mesmerizes legal associates. They daydream about it, drooling unconsciously like basset hounds remembering old soup bones.

According to associate myth, partnership is a blissful state, synonymous with heaven, paradise, nirvana, and other realms free of famine, pestilence, war, death, citechecking, and shareholder resolutions.

If this is your view, ask yourself why partners continue to leave their office lights on when they go home at night. Who are they trying to fool?

Ask yourself why partners continue to carry memos and advance sheets into the bathrooms to read at the stand-up urinals (and this isn't just the men). Who are they trying to impress?

Is something amiss in paradise?

Whether partnership will even approach your fantasies depends on a number of factors, including in particular whether your firm is large or small.

The most obvious difference between large firms and small firms is size. Hence the labels

"Welcome aboard, Witzel. You're one of us now."

"large" and "small."

But the differences don't stop there. Read on.

The Small Firm

At a small firm, making partner might have only a marginal effect on your life. Consider four key criteria.

SCUT WORK

At small firms, cases are staffed leanly as a matter of necessity, so there are limits on how much of the scut work you can get rid of.

Sure, you'll no longer have to do the scut work that doesn't have to be done by *anyone*, the absurd tasks that partners routinely make associates do simply because the associates are available and why not? But you'll have to do *some* scut work, more than enough to keep you from forgetting, when all is said and done, that you're still practicing the same law you did as an associate.

MONEY

Small firms aren't supported by a proletariat of associates who generate three times as much in client billings as they're paid. Unless you're a major-league honcho with such great connections that you can earn enough from a single well-placed phone call to buy an underdeveloped nation, or you're a plaintiff's lawyer who's lucky enough to have a shocking, horrible, nausea-inducing personal injury case roll its bent, bloodstained wheelchair into your office one day, the only yacht you'll be sailing when you make partner at a small firm is the one with the rubber-band motor that you still play with in the bathtub.

JOB SECURITY

Job security in the law is dependent on clients like I.B.M. and the Chase Manhattan Bank, which need millions of dollars worth of legal work each year. These clients have mountains of money. They print their own. They're a fantastic gravy train—but only the big firms can climb aboard.

Moreover, small firms face the constant and disastrous possibility of a split-off. What do you do if your sole expert on the one-bite rule leaves to set up his own dog-law boutique?

PRESTIGE

How great can the prestige at a small firm be? You can't dazzle

people at cocktail parties, because almost nobody will have heard of your firm. Other lawyers will snobbishly assume the competition wasn't as stiff as at the big firms.

More important, why do you care about prestige? Your friends like you because you're nice to children and you feed stray cats. People of the opposite sex like you because you can part your hair with your tongue.

The Big Firm

At a big firm, the story on partnership is different—not better, but different.

PRESTIGE

If your firm is big enough, strangers you run into at bar conventions will have heard of it. They won't necessarily be impressed, because your firm may have gotten so big that its letterhead appears to have all the exclusivity of the Publisher's Clearinghouse mailing list. But they will have heard of it.

Another reason they might not be impressed is that they will understand what you had to sacrifice to become a partner at that firm. More important, they will understand the limited nature of the benefits of partnership there.

Why "limited"? Because an essential fact of life in the big firms today is: *Partnership ain't what it used to be.*

JOB SECURITY

No longer does "partnership" equal "tenure." Less-productive partners at big firms are being forced to retire early—or just plain fired. It used to be understood that the whole point of working like a slave—the expression at big firms was "work like an associate"—was to be able, eventually, to slow down. No longer.

Life at a big firm isn't like a friendly neighborhood footrace, with separate prizes for each different age group and everyone getting together afterward for a few beers. It's more like the Olympic marathon, where there's only one division—the all-or-nothing division—and if you can't keep up with the youngest and the fastest, you're out.

Note, however, one key difference between the big-firm race and the Olympic marathon: In the big-firm race, there's no finish line. You run all-out until you die.

AUTONOMY

Well, you say, at least there's the autonomy, the control of your own destiny—surely partnership at a big firm guarantees that.

You're kidding, right?

If you picture yourself as Schlomo Sullivan (of Sullivan & Cromwell) when you fantasize about making partner, you probably also picture yourself as Caesar when you fantasize about ancient Rome. But making partner doesn't make you Caesar; it just barely gets you a bleachers seat at the Colosseum.

It's in the nature of a partnership that everything is subject to a vote. Thus, not only are you vulnerable to getting fired, but the partnership as a whole controls everything from how much vacation you get to what color carpeting you can put in your office. And in a large firm, your individual voting power is negligible.

You can't take on a new client, or even a new matter for an old client, without running it past everybody else to make sure there are no conflicts with existing work. For that matter, even if there are no conflicts, the other partners can veto your new client if they happen not to like his looks, or his politics—or his lawyer.

To add insult to injury, everything you do in a big firm is monitored and evaluated—*graded*. Is it part of your game plan to reach sixty and still be going through annual reviews not much different from the ones you feared and loathed as a young associate?

"Can I at least keep the vest and briefcase?"

MONEY

At one time a partner's pay was based largely, or even solely, on seniority. Other things being equal, more seniority meant more money.

Today you might find yourself getting *less* money with each passing year, rather than more. It just depends on how the part- nership wants to divide the pie.

Couldn't you increase your share somewhat by working a little harder in a given year? Aside from the fact that you're probably already working as hard as the human cardiovascular sys- tem can tolerate, it's up to the partnership—which might or might not choose to reward your additional labor.

Make no mistake: The money that comes with partnership at a big firm is likely to be substantial. But it's nowhere near what investment bankers make. Perhaps more relevant, the money that a brand-new partner makes isn't a great deal more than what a senior associate makes—which doesn't mean it's not enough to keep you in beer and chips, but does suggest that there's nothing magical and life-transforming on the other side of that partnership line.

THE RAINMAKER

Every lawyer wants to be a rainmaker. Rainmakers run the show.

If the other partners in a law firm don't vote the way the rainmakers want them to vote, on such essential issues as who gets the corner office and whose name goes at the top of the firm letterhead, the rainmakers can walk.

A few rainmakers bring in clients simply by being great lawyers—for example Ben White, the Atlanta-based tax mogul; Phil Feder, the bi-coastal real estate czar; and Mortimer "Bear Tracks" Snerd, Fort Worth's animal-immigration expert.

But most rainmakers get clients through personal connections and have their work done by senior associates or non-rainmaking partners.

The fact is, if you can bring in clients, you don't need to know a lot of law. You don't need to know how to read. Some rainmakers are dumber than a fundamentalist preacher.

As a rainmaker, don't you at least have to supervise the associates and non-rainmaking partners who are doing your work? Mustn't you review and edit the mountains of memoranda they turn out? There's no need. They're better at it than you are. All you have to do is sign the documents and show up at an occasional hearing—just enough to keep your clients from catching on.

*"You know, Gottlieb, the law still surges through
every inch of my being."*

The American Bar Association Convention
A Guide to Legal Personalities

"Okay, okay, so my client hacked a blind nun to pieces. But where he grew up, everybody does that."

"I feel that lawyers have a special responsibility to society. That's why I do pro bono work for Exxon."

"What a week! I've already sent three dirtbags to the Big House for life—and it's only Wednesday!"

"Did you see the new I.R.S. regs on partnership capital accounts? Fascinating!"

"Hi, good-looking. I'll bet you've got tight briefs."

"True, my briefs are concise, but you have to make every argument. Take those seventeen filings I made last week . . ."

The Public Defender: Went to NYU Law for its hip clinical program. Tortured by guilt for being born rich. Motto: "Society is to blame."

The Rainmaker: *Country club president. Married money. Wouldn't know a fee tail from a nudum pactum, but great B.S. artist. Motto: "What, me work?"*

The Prosecutor: *Grew up in tough part of New York—Manhattan. Lives to put criminal element behind bars. Motto: "Ask for the chair."*

The Tax Lawyer: *Went bald at 13. Good with numbers, but lacked the personality to be an actuary. Reads tax code during sex (alone). Motto: "Deduct or depreciate."*

The Lobbyist: *Contributes to politicians in both parties. Happy to represent highest bidder for her "contacts." Basically amoral. Motto: "What's good for my client is good for America."*

The Corporate Lawyer: *Law review editor. Young partner at New York megafirm. Had last date 3 years ago. Motto: "Sleep is dispensible."*

"Right now I'm updating my treatise on the interface of the banana-import regulations and the Uniform Commercial Code."

"Sure, judging looks easy, but believe me, these robes get hot."

"Where's the law that says all my secretaries have to be able to read?"

"Would disclosure be required if you put the stock in your dog's name and let Fido take the short-swing profits?"

"So I say to Redford, 'Rob, baby, don't sign anything without running it by me first.'"

"We'll not only sue them, we'll bury them in enough paper to wipe out a forest of giant redwoods."

The Professor: Law review editor, federal court clerk. All the social skills of a possum. Has lectured in same suit for seven years. Motto: "Anything to get published."

The Judge: Appointed after marrying governor's daughter. Can't understand why his jokes work in court but nowhere else. Likes wearing black; considered ministry for same reason. Motto: "L'etat c'est moi."

The Politico: Voted "Best Dressed Clubbie" at Princeton. Gigoloed his way through law school. Motto: "A reasonable vote for a reasonable price."

The Securities Lawyer: Former social worker. Went to law school to improve society, but sold out. Motto: "Buy low, sell high—and tell no one."

The Entertainment Lawyer: Majored in film and drugs at UCLA. Fantasizes that he's as much a celebrity as his clients. Motto: "Big! Really big!"

The Litigator: Obnoxious from birth. High school debater. Still loves to hear himself talk. Bow tie is a clip-on. Motto: "Concede nothing."

CHAPTER TEN

ELEMENTS OF STYLE: THE LAWYERLY LOOK

"My wardrobe should be as dull as my work?"

⚖

There are various points of style every lawyer should observe. For associates, these points can gain you critical mileage in the minds of that vast majority of partners who will never see your work and will know you only socially—or antisocially, as the case may be. For partners, the idea is essentially the same—there is always someone more senior you need to impress.

Dress for Legal Success

In the world of dress, formality is not synonymous with good taste. Many lawyers bear more than a passing resemblance to Lieutenant Columbo.

By and large, this doesn't matter. Lawyers rarely get out of the office, and when they do they usually just see their counterparts at other firms. Still, unless you've already given up hope for a better life, it's worthwhile to pay some attention to how you look.

MEN

Conservatism should be your sartorial guide. The rule is: "Think Yiddish, dress British." This doesn't mean you have to be stuffy. Your wardrobe of suits can run the gamut from blue to black, with even some pinstripes thrown in for a really festive touch. (The stripes should be narrower than those worn by your former clients now residing at San Quentin.)

Shirts should be white or blue. Shirts with thin pinstripes are okay, but in combination with pinstripe suits and club ties, they clash to produce a disaster à la Doc Severinsen, the "diversity suit."

Always wear a T-shirt under your white shirts. That rug on your chest may dazzle women at the beach each summer, but it looks terrible poking out between your buttons.

Shirts should generally have button-down collars. Non-button-downs are okay as long as they aren't "compass shirts," the ones with extremely long collars, one of which always sticks out as if it's trying to point north.

Ties should be narrower than the prevailing chic, whatever it is. Buy silk, not burlap. Striped ties or club ties (the ones with the silly owls or moose) are best. Avoid paisley unless you're sure you're not going to see anyone who matters. For God's sake don't get cute with one of those trompe l'oeil ties that looks like a dead fish hanging down the front of your shirt.

Pin-dot ties are okay; large polka dots are not. Especially not those ties with one huge red polka dot that spans the width of the tie and looks like it's still growing—the polka dot that ate St. Louis.

Wear a gold Cross pen in your breast pocket. It is dressy but

The Diversity Suit

sufficiently practical to pass muster in the legal context. For actual work, you'll use pencils or those wonderful felt-tip pens that let your thoughts flow like ethnic slurs at a Republican fund-raiser, but on that rare occasion when a partner or client turns to you for something with which to sign a brief or contract, you don't want to have to

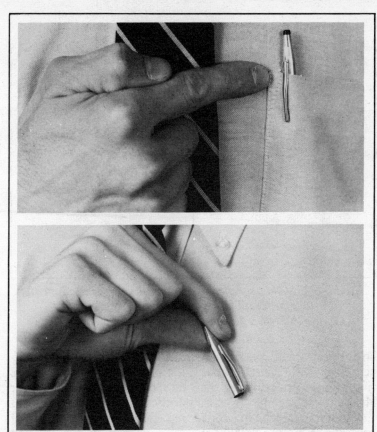

Is it—or isn't it? Oops, fooled again! When you're wearing this simulated 14K. gold Cross pen (available at fine jewelry stores everywhere), partners and clients will never suspect that it isn't the real thing projecting proudly from your breast pocket, ever ready to execute a multimillion-dollar contract. For just $9.95 (plus $2.50 shipping and handling), you can acquire the look of success, even though you can barely cover the installments on your mail-order suit from Hong Kong. Remember: In the law, appearances are everything!

fish through your trouser pockets, only to come up with a tooth-marred Bic with lint balls caught in the clip.

Jewelry is best avoided, par-

ticularly gold medallions, unless you actually want people to know you grew up in Brooklyn. The same goes for huge diamond rings, unless you were

Your coiffure should reflect the preferred legal temperament: uptight! Don't let your hair down—and show the real *you—until you've left the office.*

on the team that won the Super Bowl. Ditto for all pinkie rings, unless you represent the Mafia.

As for your watch, you don't need one so big and flashy that it looks like you're wearing Fort Knox—or so big and ugly that people assume you need to be able to tell time seven miles underwater. And stay away from those silly jogging watches, even if you've long felt that black plastic is underrated as a dress item.

WOMEN

Except at some of the stuffiest firms in New York (which is to say, "Except at some of the stuffiest places in the world"), it is now okay for women to wear dresses rather than suits. This represents progress. Until recent years women in the law felt compelled to look like men. Now they only feel compelled to *act* like men.

Otherwise, the rules of drabness are the same. Your attire should match your job. Makeup should be minimized and perfume avoided altogether. You don't want to encourage the senior partner to think of you in the same vein as the women he knew in Paris during the war.

Hemlines should stay at or below the knees (or partners' eyes

"The jig is up. Mr. Cobb found out that the briefcase I so diligently carry home each night contains my gym clothes."

won't). Shun dresses with slits up the sides unless (a) you have great legs, and (b) you're bucking for promotion to receptionist.

Your hairstyle should be inconspicuous, preferably gathered up in a wad in the back. Anything too ornate will give the impression that you spend a lot of time fussing with it when you could be practicing law. This is better from your perspective as well; practicing law, like having a baby, puts a major premium on quick-and-easy.

Shoe heels should be low, if not flat. It's impossible to look dignified when you're stranded in a subway grating. Also, high heels will cause people to confuse you with secretaries (who aren't bucking for partnership and therefore feel free to dress as uncomfortably as they like).

Large breasts should be avoided. Partners will stare.

The Briefcase

Carry a large one. No *business* person would be caught dead carrying a large briefcase—someone *else* handles his grunt work —but lawyers *thrive* on grunt work. Senior partners take pride in walking out of their offices on Friday night with two briefcases, each big enough to hold a human body.

Carrying a large briefcase is part of cultivating the proper image. You needn't have anything in it, although an article or manuscript is handy in case a senior partner sits so close on the bus one morning that she might notice if you're reading (or drooling over) *Sports Illustrated*.

Office Props

Subscribe to the *Harvard Law Review*. People outside your firm will rarely remember what law school you went to, and they will *never* remember whether you were on that school's Law Review. If you store your issues

U.S. Chief Justice William ("I swear it's only medicine for my back pain") Rehnquist

on a center shelf of your office (particularly *bound* volumes for the years when you were actually in the YMCA night law program), people will assume you attended Harvard and made Law Review there.

This is a safe trick, because if challenged, you can always claim you're just trying to stay abreast of developments in the law. It is not unduly expensive, because you only need two years' worth to achieve the desired effect.

This is somewhat akin to hanging a picture of a Supreme Court justice* on your wall to make everyone think you clerked for that justice. If challenged, you can reply that you just happen to admire that justice a great deal—a reasonable defense unless you've forged on it a personal inscription to yourself.

---

*A *real* Supreme Court justice—not one of those frauds on the New York trial court.

REAL LAWYERS EAT FAST FOOD

A J.D. degree and a passed bar exam do not a *real* lawyer make. There's more to being a real lawyer—such as messing up sentences by reversing the subject and predicate (*see* preceding sentence).

How can you tell if you're a real lawyer, an Arnold Schwarzenegger of a lawyer? Measure yourself by the following criteria:

1. *Real lawyers eat fast food.* The faster, the better—and preferably something you can eat at your desk. Eating just gets in the way of work.

2. *Real lawyers don't have tans.* They prefer the library to the beach; it's tough to draft a prospectus lying in the sand.

3. *Real lawyers don't drive flashy cars.* Rainmakers might, but nobody said they're real lawyers. Real lawyers aren't into style and pizzazz.

4. *Real lawyers don't have beards.* Not even the men. Beards are bushy and untidy. Even a mustache looks too much like nose hairs grown out of control.

5. *Real lawyers work on Sundays. Lots* of lawyers go in on Saturdays; that's expected. Only the hard guys can bear it on Sundays, when the ventilation has been off for two days and the air smells so ripe you'd swear it's wearing your old college roommate's gym socks.

6. *Real lawyers don't have erotic daydreams.* They don't have trouble concentrating on their work. For a real lawyer, tax reports are enough to arouse his attention.

7. *Real lawyers love to proofread—everything.* Not just legal documents and formal correspondence. Real lawyers proofread street signs, magazine ads, menus, even the little placards under fish tanks at the local aquarium. Nothing makes their day like catching a typo.

8. *Real lawyers don't like children.* Children are noisy, frivolous, distracting. Kids just don't care about the important things in life—class actions, Rule 10b-5, mitigation of damages.

CHAPTER ELEVEN

ALTERNATIVE ROUTES: GOVERNMENT SERVICE, COUNTRY LAW

⚖

Private practice in an urban law factory isn't the only route. Some of the finest lawyers around opt for government service—or head for the hills.

The Government Lawyer

The primary distinction of government practice is early, hands-on responsibility—none of these four-year warm-up periods before getting to argue some piddling motion for extension of time in a district court.

A government salary is nothing to write home about, particularly in comparison with what some lawyers make in private practice. But if you measure income in dollars *per hour*, it's far from clear who comes out on top.

If private firms spawned the concept of the twenty-five-hour workday, government practice spawned the concept of the twenty-five-hour work *week*.

Government practice might be right for you—no private firm ever served a bigger client —but don't make any rash decisions. Read the following rules on survival as a government lawyer to be sure you know what you're getting into:

1. *Make sure you have your own desk.* Nothing is certain in government employ-

ment. It is too much to hope for a private office, but demand your own desk. In fact, negotiate this before you accept the job.

2. *Hone your secretarial skills.* If you got through law school without knowing how to type, now is the time to learn.

Some good news and some bad news. The good news is that word processing machines and related equipment are not beyond the technical competence of a highly trained professional like yourself. The bad news is that there's a reason they're so simple. Read on.

There are a number of fine secretaries in the government (people debate whether the number is two or three), but you will not get one right off the bat—say, within your first decade. You will get another kind, to whom filing his or her fingernails is more important than filing your briefs.

Do not be too harsh in judging these secretaries. They work under trying conditions—handling five lawyers' briefs and correspondence between ten and three-thirty, with two hours out for lunch, *All My Children*, and *The Young and the Restless.** In judging them, consider that your own output would suffer if you wore Sony Walk-Man earphones all day.

Secretarial self-reliance is essential to government practice. You don't have to be able to take apart and reassemble a Xerox 2000-X copier—but it wouldn't hurt. You will invariably be the next person to use a machine after someone has dropped a box of paper clips into its guts. Note: When the lights start blinking, do not panic—leave quietly and find another machine.

3. *Dress functionally.* Dress is not as important in the government as in private practice. A government salary can't support a fancy wardrobe, and let's face it, who wants to wear a $700 suit sitting behind a metal desk?

4. *Avoid drift.* The pace of government practice can be casual and pleasant, to say the least. You will undoubtedly be tempted, on a prolonged basis, to relax, settle back, borrow your secretary's Sony Walk-Man, and give no thought to the future.

Resist this temptation!

You're there to learn and

---

*These strains can result in unconscious editorial contributions to your work product. True story: A lawyer who dictated the sentence "Refer the matter to the Criminal Division" got back for his signature a neatly typed letter reading "Refer that mother to the Criminal Division." Always proofread your work.

Cherry regulations—Drafting these could be the end of the line.

that are transferrable to the private sector, e.g., litigation or securities. Reviewing documents under the Freedom of Information Act might seem interesting for two days, maybe three—but a year of it could turn you into a government lawyer forever.

The Country Lawyer

The joy of being a country lawyer, like that of being a country doctor, is that you're also part psychologist, part family therapist, and maybe part plumber and animal midwife.

The *problem* with being a country lawyer is that you have to live in the country, which requires learning to whittle, chew tobacco, and spit. Otherwise, people won't cotton to you.

Depending on your tastes, country life might not be so bad. Think of baseball players—they *love* chewing tobacco. (Of course, for their salaries there's nothing you wouldn't chew.) You might not get off on the sight of your partner making functional use of the spittoon at the foot of his desk every fifteen minutes, but who's to say that's worse than being told to perform anatomically impossible acts on yourself in a New York subway each morning. (If

advance, not drift. Government practice has a thousand dead ends—*somebody* has to write those regulations governing the labeling of cherry pits—and you don't want to find yourself stranded.

Don't assume it will be obvious when your career has come to a halt. Unlike the private sector, the government doesn't operate on an up-or-out system. You might be doing the same thing in thirty years that you did when you began. (If you doubt that this will affect your mental acuity, try carrying on a conversation with the "lifer" at the end of the hall.)

At a minimum, learn skills

GOVERNMENT TRAVEL

If the government has billions to spend on Patriot missiles, a lot of that comes from what it *doesn't* spend on its legal staff. A military force as poorly equipped as the average government legal division couldn't mount a successful panty raid on a girl's prep school.

The government's miserly policies toward its own are most apparent when it comes to travel. Government lawyers travel a good bit. The big guns in Washington don't feel comfortable leaving important cases to the local crew in places like Iowa. Can you blame them?

The government lawyer who has to fly somewhere is usually surprised to learn that there is a class lower than coach—and he may be in trouble if he's allergic to animals. Also, the government would prefer that he kill two days city-hopping between Washington and St. Louis rather than spend an extra forty dollars for a direct flight. (This makes sense: Given the tightwad government per diem, they'd save money even if it took a week.)

The government lawyer on the road doesn't have a wide array of hotel options. If he's not crashing on a friend's sofa, he's staying at one of the orange-roofed Johnson establishments. While his counterparts in private practice are limousining around town in search of haute cuisine on which to squander client funds, the government lawyer considers himself lucky to find an all-beef patty within walking distance of his room.

the mugger is armed, you may find the acts aren't impossible.)

The major difference between the practice of a big-city lawyer and that of a country lawyer or even suburban lawyer is the level of perfection that goes into the work. Big-city lawyers do a perfect job on every project, no matter how disproportionate the costs of a perfect job are to the stakes involved. They'll not only produce an eighty-page lease for a one-bedroom apartment, but also spend thousands of dollars proofreading the eighty-page lease.

Country and suburban lawyers can't do this. Their clients are individuals or small companies (Tuscaloosa Grits and Radial Tires, Inc.) who just can't afford it. For this reason country and suburban lawyers have to do something that big-city lawyers never have to do: pull in the reins, perform cost-benefit analysis—exercise *judgment*.

Note: It's easy enough to become a country lawyer. Just drive into the country and hang up a shingle: "Suits pressed."

However, if you're planning to become a country lawyer in the South, your first priority should be to buy a King James version of the Bible and master the use of words like "thence," "forsook," and "begat." Ever since North Carolinian Sam Ervin's performance in the Senate Watergate hearings, it's expected—no less than being able to put down a whole plateful of collards and possum with a smile.

U.S. Sen. Sam Ervin, Jr.— Country lawyer. Connoisseur of possum. Encyclopedic knowledge of Holy Scriptures.

CHAPTER TWELVE

WOMEN IN THE LAW

Subpoena Envy?

⚖

You don't have to wear briefs to write them. Most law schools these days are fifty percent or more female, and the summer programs and entering classes at the major law firms are the same.*

But what about where the big money is, at the partnership level in the big firms? Here, too, we see change: No longer do they hold partnership meetings in locker rooms, where the older guys used to like wandering around naked, popping one another with rolled-up towels, and calling each other things like "you old scrotum-head."

For those of you discouraged by the distance that remains between the reality and the ideal, there may also be comfort in knowing that male lawyers are nowhere near as bad as, say, construction workers or Congressmen. This is due not only to the emasculating aspects of the law school experience, but also to the brutal hours most lawyers put in: As with prisoners of war, their carnal urges take a backseat to the demands of food and sleep.

Interestingly, a few lawyers respond in the opposite way, becoming sexually omnivorous, hitting on anyone and every-

*This has all happened over the past thirty years. Fewer than 2,200 women, or four percent of the total law school population, were enrolled in accredited law schools in 1964. A decade later the number had increased to 21 percent. The female share passed the one-third mark in 1981, and as of 1991 the lines at the women's restrooms in law schools were easily three times as long as the men's.

one, in the indiscriminate manner of sharks munching on the dangling legs of passengers from a just capsized Cunard liner (a thought that should in no way influence your next choice of a vacation).

But even these legal lechers aren't on a par with the other groups mentioned above, for the simple reasons that lawyers are less likely to persist in the face of rejection. They know too well the possibility of a sex-discrimination lawsuit. Also, as veterans of social rejection—most

lawyers have been encountering it since infancy—they know better than to hope to overcome it.

True, a few old codgers still find the time and energy to nurture their fear of competition from women. They ask, "If women are so equal, why is Barbara Mikulski so short?"

But even these diehards grow mute when confronted with the existence of Dan Quayle—a living, breathing rebuttal of the myth of male superiority.

In any event, the times, they

"So you went to law school and now you want to practice law. I think that's cute."

U.S. Justice Sandra Day O'Connor

are a'changin (to a'quote a'Bob a'Dylan, a'from a'Italy). Women are moving into all areas of the law, proving slowly but surely that they can be every bit as dull and compulsive as men.

The Supreme Court ruled in a case involving a big Atlanta firm that lawyers may not discriminate against women in de-ciding who makes partner. And at least one such case has gone to trial, resulting in a decision that the defendant law firm, a sizable Philadelphia operation, was not only guilty of discrimination against women, but criminally tacky. That firm is now in what George Bush—it may have been Millard Fillmore—

called "deep doo-doo."

The Supreme Court itself now includes one woman, Sandra Day O'Connor, who got on that august body because she deserved to be there, not because SHE WAS FOOLING AROUND WITH ED MEESE. And let it be said right here and now that no one connected with this book wants anything to do with perpetuating that kind of sleazy, sexist rumor—no matter what those photographs show.

Finally, and perhaps most important, women in business schools are excelling. Over time women will run the companies that will become the clients of women in the law. When women become rainmakers, their success in the law is assured—at which point the only question will be whether they'll start popping one another with rolled up towels and calling each other "you old scrotum-head."

HOW IS A WOMAN TO COPE?

In any law firm with partners old enough to have gray hair (or no hair), a woman will at least occasionally encounter "traditional" attitudes. There are three basic strategies in response:

1. *The Crusader.* A sort of scorched-earth approach, this involves addressing every single offense or inequity, without regard to size or context. The main problem with this strategy is that it requires so much energy. It's a noble battle, but exhausting.

2. *The Mata Hari.* A few women, motivated by frustration or contempt (or both), undertake to exploit those feminine resources that male partners appear most willing to recognize and reward. You can spot a hard-core Mata Hari by her black mesh stockings and garter belt.

3. *The Survivor.* This pragmatic approach consists of equal parts diplomacy, competence, thick skin, and strong sense of humor: "Sure, I'll get you some coffee, Mr. Mernick—if you'll pick up some tampons for me when you go to lunch." It combines traces of Katharine Hepburn-like insouciance and Margaret Mead-like tolerance of primates who are about as high on the evolutionary ladder as professional hockey players. It involves not letting your core values feel threatened in situations that require you to endure, say, a conversation about sports. Who knows?—you may like sports.

The Mata Hari. *A dazzling effect,*
but will the court be able to
keep its learned hands off her fee tail?

The Bush Administration Shows Lawyers the Way

Who can forget Donald Regan, President Reagan's amiable chief of staff and the pioneering social thinker who opined that women could hardly be expected (or allowed) to play a role in formulating American foreign policy, because the little dears don't know the first thing about missile "throw weight"—which guys of course pick up naturally, through the same innate scientific curiosity that leads them to chug twenty-seven beers in ten minutes and then see who can vomit the farthest?

True, quite a few people would *like* to forget Regan, and to this extent you have to envy President Reagan, who has forgotten everything from around the time of the Iran-contra scandal and going at least ten years in both directions from there. Still, some things linger indefinitely—like the doggie poop that gets into the crevices of your sneakers and won't come out no matter how many times you rub them in the grass or bang them on the sidewalk, and you end up having to leave them outside so they won't smell up the house.

Researchers for this book have turned up the following White House memo, which demonstrates that the spirit of Donald Regan lives on:

MEMORANDUM FROM THE WHITE HOUSE

To: Lawyers Doing Business with the Bush Administration
Re: Gyno-Americans in the Legal Profession

We at the Bush White House originally planned to continue Don Regan's policy of ultra-sensitivity to women's issues, but in the seventeen seconds since you began reading this memo, our plans have changed. It is now our official policy that ... no, wait ... all right, we're back to the original approach. Okay, *this* is our policy, and we're going to stick by it for at least as long as it takes you to read to the bottom of this page.

Gals have, of course, entered the legal profession in droves. Apparently they don't give a damn what happens to their children, or maybe they're gay and don't have any—who knows? Whatever, at a firm of any size you're sure to find yourself working shoulder to shoulder-pad with several, and you'd better conduct yourself appropriately. This is especially true if you aspire to an actual position with the Bush Administration or ... giggle, chuckle, smirk (hey, *you* try saying this with a straight face) ... the Quayle Administration.

RULES

1. Avoid the term "girl lawyer." This seems to give offense, probably because the kind of females who go into the law wish, deep down, they were guys. Whatever, the proper term is "lady lawyer."

2. Do not ask a lady lawyer to get you coffee or tea. Ask her to ask your *secretary* to get it. This wastes a little time, but it keeps them both quiet, so what the hell.

3. If you ever slip and say "hell" or "damn" in front of a lady lawyer, apologize immediately and let her know you don't expect her to be able to handle such rough language.

4. In recruiting, do not ask a female applicant about her plans for marriage or children. It is okay, however, to ask what type of birth control she uses and whether she's wearing a bra.

5. Remember that a little tasteful levity can generate valuable goodwill. Acceptable topics for jokes these days include lesbian motherhood and the size of female breasts.

6. When you and the other guys at the firm meet for drinks, poker, or softball, do your female colleagues the courtesy of letting them know about the event afterward. Emphasize the extent to which firm matters were discussed, so they'll know their interests were being looked after.

7. Most lady lawyers will of course be happiest doing matrimonial or trusts-and-estates work. You should indulge a few of those requesting litigation, however, because who knows when one of your cases will come before a lady judge? (Obviously you

shouldn't use your more attractive lady lawyers for this purpose, because what are the chances a lady judge will rule for someone who's trimmer or prettier than she is?)

8. In speaking with a lady judge, use the standard "Your Honor" form of address—as in "Is it Your Honor's time of the month?"

9. This respectful attitude should be maintained at the appellate level. For example, "The Court below was clearly approaching *its* time of the month." Or even—to demonstrate your sensitivity to the problem of sexist language—"The trial judge was clearly approaching *his or her* time of the month."

10. If a lady lawyer should express interest in working on a jury trial, take the time to explain that women simply aren't aggressive enough for such work, that the softness and innate passivity which makes them so charming renders them unsuited to the courtroom. (What about the rare woman who's every bit as aggressive as a man? Let her exploit her feminine wiles elsewhere—maybe with Martina on the pro tennis circuit. You want the jurors concentrating on your case, not speculating on your co-counsel's chromosomes.)

11. It is of course tempting to date someone at your own firm, because you don't have to pick her up, and the whole thing is tax-deductible. To avoid the appearance of sexual favoritism, however, first you must have her fired. We know this seems harsh, asking you to go to all that trouble just to avoid the appearance of impropriety, but such are the burdens of membership in the fraternity of the law.

CHAPTER THIRTEEN

LEGAL WRITING

"Excuse me, but what does this say in English?"

⚖

Everyone knows that legal writing is different from regular writing. People can understand regular writing.

Legal writing is instantly recognizable. There's no mistaking a "whereas" or a "forthwith." You can spot an "anything herein to the contrary notwithstanding" a mile away. (Talk about floccinaucinihilipilification.)

Why do lawyers write this way? Several reasons.

First, they like big words. Lots of people like big words, but dealing with them ten to twelve hours a day affects your brain, altering your perspective on what is a sesquipedalian and what isn't.

A lawyer will say "automobile" when he could say "car," and he'll say "mass transporta-tion vehicle" when he could say "bus." He'll even say "practicable" when he means "practical." No one outside the law has ever heard of the word "practicable."

The second trait that makes lawyers write so peculiarly is that they are exceedingly meticulous—anal—by nature. This translates into an unnatural craving for precision in their prose, notwithirregardlessly respecting which they don't always succeed—but they try.

The third trait that accounts for lawyers' bizarre writing style is innate conservatism. The average lawyer is not bold by nature. His ambition is to go through life with his ass fully covered. To this end he qualifies everything he writes, in-

*"Bunnen, find me authority for the proposition
that the law is an ass."*

stinctively fearful of being caught in an exaggeration, or even a metaphor.

The lawyer will tell you it's his client he's trying to protect, or that he's just trying to preserve his credibility in the eyes of the judge. This is about as accurate as the claim that he's wearing a vest to keep warm.

"THE SKY IS BLUE"

These stylistic peculiarities are particularly evident in the man-

ner in which partners edit the writing of associates.

Every partner fancies himself a grammarian. He would edit Strunk & White. There is no sentence so straightforward and simple that he will not happily torture it beyond recognition.

Take the sentence "The sky is blue."

Please.

No junior associate would be so naive as to think this proposition could pass muster in a big firm. If he made it through law school he knows enough to say, "The sky is *generally* blue."

Better yet, "The sky generally *appears* blue."

For extra syllables, "The sky generally appears *to be* blue."

A senior associate seeing this sentence might take pity on the junior associate and explain that before showing it to a partner, the junior associate should put in a more "lawyerly" form. At the very least, the sentence should be revised to say, "In some parts of the world, what is generally thought of as the sky sometimes appears to be blue."

Armed with these qualifiers, the junior associate thinks himself protected.

His conversation with the reviewing partner will proceed thus:

PARTNER CARTER: You say here that in some parts of the world, what is generally thought of as the sky sometimes appears to be blue. I assume this is just an early draft. Could I see the final version?

ASSOCIATE WILLIAMS: Uh, that's all I have right now . . . what exactly do you mean?

PARTNER CARTER: Well, it's a bit bald, don't you think? I mean, just to come out and assert it as fact.

ASSOCIATE WILLIAMS: I beg your pardon? Are we talking about the same thing?

PARTNER CARTER: Well, this busi-

"SPEAKING AS A LAWYER . . ."

Lawyers commonly preface their remarks with "Speaking as a lawyer . . ." Is this a boast? A disclaimer?

Whatever else it is, it's unnecessary. It's *obvious* when someone is "speaking as a lawyer."

For one thing, lawyers over-enunciate their words, smacking their lips and pronouncing each syllable crisply and distinctly, as if talking to someone for whom English isn't a native tongue.

This can be irritating. Sometimes it makes you want to insert their tongues into the office paper shredder.

Lawyers also talk in uncommonly full, formal sentences. They take pains to select just the right words for their thoughts, as if they're talking on the record—for posterity.

A lot posterity cares.

ness about the sky—what did you mean by the sky?

ASSOCIATE WILLIAMS: Well, I meant what I see when I look up . . . at least, when I'm outside. Isn't that what everyone sees?

PARTNER CARTER: Okay, if you mean *only* when you're outside, you have to say so. Our opponents in this case would love to rip us apart on that kind of error. And what about at night? Even at night? I see stars at night—are they blue? Do you mean everything *but* stars, or do you mean when there are no stars out?

ASSOCIATE WILLIAMS: I meant during the day, I guess.

PARTNER CARTER: You *guess*. Williams, this is serious business. We can't go around guessing at things. Besides, what about the sun? If it's daytime, the sun will be out —or do you know something I don't?

ASSOCIATE WILLIAMS: Well, sure . . . I mean, no, I don't . . . but no one in his right mind looks at the sun. You'd go blind.

PARTNER CARTER: What support do you have for this comment about "some parts of the world"? *Which* parts? Do we need to start it so broadly? Can't we just say "in Cleveland" or wherever we mean?

ASSOCIATE WILLIAMS: That sounds fine to me. I just never thought anyone would challenge . . . that is, who would disagree with . . .

PARTNER CARTER: And what do you mean by "generally thought of"? Thought of by whom? Lawyers? Scientists? Morticians? Dammit, Williams, this piece has more holes in it than Swiss cheese. I haven't seen such sloppiness in all my years at Cavil, Quibble & Quiver. Take it back and see if you can't do a little better this time around.

Even more startling for new associates than this distortion of English by verbally incontinent old-timers is the process by which legal briefs are written.

Law students are taught that judges decide cases on the basis of previous cases, that the system is ruled by precedent. Accordingly, they assume that the way lawyers write briefs is by researching previous cases and constructing arguments based on those cases.

What really happens is that partners or senior associates write the briefs *first*. They know what they want to say; they know how their argument has to come out.

Then they turn the brief over to a junior associate, with each assertion followed by a brack-

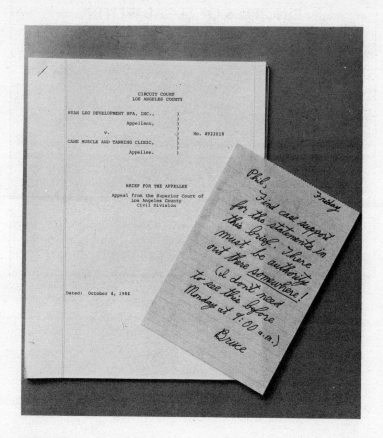

eted note: "[Find case support for this statement.]"*

This process obviously assumes that there is case support out there for any proposition. There is.

*Every firm's history includes at least one story of a new recruit fired for failing to catch all of these references in the final brief. For some reason, judges get upset when they find remarks like "[Cite usual crap.]"

What about those few propositions so well hidden that they cannot be located even by the army of associates that big firms will readily commit to the search?

You do with these propositions what Thomas Jefferson—a lawyer—did with the proposition "all men are created equal": You put them up front and call them "self-evident."

PRINCIPLES OF LEGAL WRITING

1. Never use one word where ten will do.
2. Never use a small word where a big one will do suffice.
3. Never use a simple statement where it appears that one of substantially greater complexity will achieve comparable goals.
4. Never use English where Latin, *mutatis mutandis*, will do.
5. Qualify virtually everything.
6. Do not be embarrassed about repeating yourself.
7. Do not be embarrassed about repeating yourself.
8. Worry about the difference between "which" and "that."
9. Never refer to your opponent's "arguments"—he makes only "assertions," and his assertions are always "bald."
10. If a lay person can read a document from beginning to end without falling asleep, it needs work.

CHAPTER FOURTEEN

DRAFTING LEGAL DOCUMENTS: CONTRACTS, LEASES, WILLS

More is better—unless it begins to make sense.

⚖

"Legal writing" is different from "legal drafting." Lawyers use the former term to refer to briefs, letters, and memoranda, but they like to say they "draft" contracts, leases and wills. "Draft" suggests refined skills, even artistic capabilities.

Drafting truly impenetrable documents is not easy. Many young lawyers' initial attempts at legal drafting are rejected outright, with senior partners offering such helpful comments as "This won't do. I can still get the gist of some of the sentences."

Fortunately for young lawyers, most kinds of documents have been drafted hundreds, even thousands of times before. The large law firms have countless file drawers full of old documents, and the associate who is asked to draft, say, an industrial revenue bond needs merely to rummage through the files for an old one that looks about right.

A paralegal could do it. Paralegals *do* do it.

Solo practitioners and lawyers in small firms don't have it much harder. There are hundreds of commercially sold "mumbo-jumbo books," with model contracts, leases, and wills of every imaginable sort.

If your client is a Hindu who wants to leave all his posses- sions to his sacred cow, the mumbo-jumbo books have several versions of the form you need. Just fill in the name and address of the cow.

TYPES OF LEGAL DOCUMENTS

Fundamentally, there are only four types of legal documents:

1. boring;
2. extremely boring;
3. comatose; and
4. pull-the-plug-and-let-me-die-with-dignity.

There are four types of lawyers who produce these documents:

1. boring;
2. extremely boring;
3. comatose; and
4. those for whom the plug has been pulled.

(The last are easy to spot—they're the ones with all the dignity.)

Notwithstanding this simplicity at one level, legal documents come in a dazzling array. Whether you need something to paper over a deal or, more important, to put under the short leg of a sofa, you have an impressive smorgasbord to choose from.

In part this reflects the complexity of modern transactions, in part lawyers' zeal for their trade. It also reflects the rabbit-like procreative powers of legal documents: Left alone in a drawer at night, leases beget subleases, wills beget trusts, deeds beget mortgages, debentures beget subordinated convertibles—with a fecundity of biblical proportions.

Thus far the only known form of birth control is a client who refuses to pay his legal bill—which reveals in yet another context the merit of learning to "just say no."

How to Draft a Contract from Scratch

Legal writing requires a great deal of skill on those rare occasions when the client wants to do something that has never been done before. Then you can't rely on old forms; you have to obfuscate on your own.

In such situations, you proceed thus:

First, describe in normal language whatever it is the client wants to do. Then lengthen it.

A good way to begin the lengthening process is to make express provision for every conceivable turn of events, no matter how remote. Be sure to describe which party to the contract is at risk if an outbreak of malaria among Indonesian cane harvesters jeopardizes the Kentucky market for thoroughbred foals, particularly if the contract deals with office space in Seattle.

Continue the lengthening process by defining the obvious and qualifying the irrelevant.

With regard to definitions, do not hesitate to define things in improbable ways. A good lawyer feels no compunction about defining "person" to mean "corporations, partnerships, and livestock"; "automobile" to mean "airplanes, submarines, and bi-cycles"; and "cash" to mean "stocks, bonds, and whiskey."

Do not stop with hundreds of useless definitions and qualifications. Go through it again and again, expanding clauses and inserting redundancies. This will enable you to avoid the perils of certain forms of punctuation, notably as the period.

Once you have revised your original description to the point that no one without a Ph.D. in semantics and sophistry could understand it, the next step is to break it down into numerous paragraphs, sub-paragraphs, and sub-sub-paragraphs, ad infinitum. This way the various units can refer back and forth to each other ("as provided hereinabove in subsection 43d-4/(g)(1)(A)(viii), except for sub-part Q-3(a) thereof . . ."), thus eliminating any hint of continuity or readability.

By the time you've completed these steps, your contract should defy analysis by Japanese cryptologists. All that remains is to add a few "exhibits," "attachments," and "appendices." These don't have to be relevant to anything; they're for bulk—roughage for your legal digestive track.

The height of the art is to have an attachment to an exhibit to an appendix, with cross-references to documents not even included.

DRAFTING AND PUNCTUATION: THE PERILS OF PERIODS

A period marks the end of a sentence. This is clearly understood. For this reason periods should be avoided. Commas, too, tend to clarify rather than obfuscate.

But the indeterminacy of colons and semicolons lets them mean anything you want (which is not to say you have to let the reader in on your secret). With colons and semicolons, sentences can be extended indefinitely; subjects can be separated from predicates by pages numbering in the double figures.

Dashes and parentheticals, if properly employed, can yield a nicely convoluted sentence. But God only knows the proper use and meaning of a colon. And a semicolon is just half of that.

Far more important than anything you say in a document is whether you are consistent in your use of letters, numbers, and Roman numerals. The same lawyers and judges who view a readable contract as beneath contempt become distraught upon encountering a bungled cross-reference forward or backward.

Revising documents is therefore fraught with danger. If you eliminate or, more likely, add a single clause or paragraph early on, all subsequent numbers and letters are thrown out of kilter.

This is why you see so many amendments and addenda located at the *end* of legal documents. Lawyers are mortally afraid of screwing up the numbers.

A WORD OF WARNING

Never do two opposing lawyers sit down and draft a contract together. One side takes a first crack at it, the other side studies the product, and then they duke it out.

If you're not the lawyer who produced the initial draft, remember: The most dangerous part of a contract is not what's in it, but what's *not* in it.

An export agreement with no choice-of-law provision could have you arguing your client's next breach-of-contract case in Bulgaria. An artificial-insemination agreement that doesn't say what happens if the big bovine proves to be a little light in his loafers could have you testing your powers of advocacy in a barn (possibly a barn in Bulgaria).

Two related points: (1) The initial draft produced by the opposing lawyer will generally work just fine, assuming nothing goes wrong. (2) Something will go wrong.

Sometimes, to be sure, the contract will prove irrelevant—where one side has gone belly-up, for example, or both sides have breached the contract in a thousand different ways, or both sides realize that the litigation would go on so long that only their grandchildren would be around for the final ruling. These kinds of situations may let you get away with letting the other side's lawyer get away with omitting key provisions.

In other situations, however, the contract could prove critical. For these you'd better have made sure it has everything it ought to have—or you may leave the firm without everything *you* ought to have.

Legal Machismo: The Running of the Pen at Pamplona

Lawyers say words are their stock in trade. If so, they are bur-

---

AMONG V. BETWEEN

A lawyer who doesn't know the difference between "among" and "between" has missed his true calling as a bricklayer.

Until you have time to delve into this difficult but fascinating area on your own, you may be able to get by with the following rule of thumb: When the parties to a contract number three or more, the contract should recite that it is entered "by and *among*" the parties. When the parties number fewer than three (usually two), the contract should recite that it is entered "by and *between*" the parties.

Why it is not enough to say simply that the contract is entered "by" the parties is an issue going to the very heart of the law.

THE MYTH OF
THE REASONABLE CONTRACT

Contracts, leases, and the like are not neutral documents. Lawyers draft them for specific clients, and their terms invariably favor the client of the lawyer who drafted them.

A lease drafted by a landlord's lawyer, for example, will provide for late fees if the tenant doesn't pay his rent on time, and capital punishment if it happens twice.

The same lease drafted by a tenant's lawyer will give the tenant a twenty-day grace period for tardy payments and provide for apologies by the tenant if he doesn't pay by then.

So one-sided are most documents that lawyers' form files often contain two versions of each type of contract, one version drafted for one side, one version for the other. The lawyers could just as easily swap sides and use the other versions sitting in their files.

What goes on in contract negotiations is, the lawyers sit around identifying and complaining about the outrageous provisions in each other's proposals, until ultimately they come up with a reasonable document. The virtue of this process is that it enables each side's lawyer to give the appearance of driving a hard bargain—and then to charge an enormous fee.

dened by an excess of inventory.

Why are lawyers enamored of length in their documents? Partly, no doubt, because most lawyers are men, and men have always been enamored of length —a phenomenon presumably traceable to the sense of inadequacy experienced by every young boy as he contemplates the superior weaponry of his father as Oedipal competitor. But that's for another book.

There's a touch of Heming-way in everyone. But lawyers can't run with the bulls or go deep-sea fishing, so they find surrogate manhood—and this includes the women—in their papers.

They deny the desk-bound tameness of their lives by conceiving of their documents as weapons of battle. A lawyer refers to a contract of which he's particularly proud as "bullet-proof," meaning it can hold up under even the closest judicial scrutiny. He speaks of "hammering" his opponents with a forceful brief, or "nailing them to the wall" with a fiercely worded motion.

This button-down, white-collar brand of cojones finds its most comical expression in the pride lawyers take in the length of their documents. A lawyer boasts of a three-hundred-page contract the way a sportsman boasts of a three-hundred-pound fish. He'll show a two-hundred-page brief to his family and friends like a little boy showing off the hole he dug in the backyard.

The difference is that the three-hundred-pound fish and the hole in the backyard didn't cost anyone thousands of dollars.

Also, if you thought about it for a long time, you could probably find something socially useful about the hole and the fish.

CHAPTER FIFTEEN

LAWYERS AND HUMOR

There are no funny lawyers—only funny people who made a career mistake.

⚖

When big firm corporate lawyers claim their work benefits society as a whole, you have to wonder who's writing their material. These are funny guys!

Lawyers are not known for their scintillating wit, however. On the contrary, they are perceived as humorless, sober, and drab—and for this reason are frequently mistaken for Baptists.

The perception of lawyers as humorless is not entirely their fault. It is due in part to the nature of the occasions that cause people to consult lawyers. You don't go to a lawyer for a periodic checkup, the way you do your auto mechanic or gynecologist (who, by the way,

should be two different people). You go to a lawyer for a divorce, an auto wreck, an I.R.S. audit—things that seldom put you in the mood for mirth.

Moreover, who can be humorous when he's exhausted and fully prepared to do a facedown in his dinner? A lawyer at the end of the week is like a marathoner on his twenty-sixth mile—tired and smelly.

The fact that lawyers are not the *source* of much humor does not mean they cannot enjoy a good joke told by someone else. Lawyers laugh long and hard at jokes told by judges, wealthy clients, and I.R.S. examiners. Lawyers may not *know* many

When judges joke, lawyers laugh.

jokes, but they are able to *appreciate* jokes—on any subject but themselves.

Actually, associates in large law firms are no more humorless than the public at large. Given the comical nature of most of what associates do (and

all of what they bill), it is surprising that more professional comedians do not emerge from their ranks. Charging $225 per hour for proofreading documents breeds an acute sense of the absurd.

The most peculiar aspect of

humor in the life of associates is the extent to which they must confine it to other associates. Partners who have been known to laugh—*out loud*—in response to jokes told by other partners show a remarkable reluctance to acknowledge humor out of the mouths of associates.

This behavior could reflect a conscious effort to impress young lawyers with the seriousness of the firm's work. It could also reflect partners' revulsion at the thought of how associates spend their time—not an unreasonable response.

Most likely it reflects a psychological defense mechanism. Partners don't want to grow too intimate with people who by all odds will be compelled to leave the firm after expending their finest energies. This phenomenon resembles the reluctance felt by jailers in ancient Rome to become familiar with prisoners about to face the lions.

Legal Graffiti

There once was a lawyer
  named Rex,
Whose "thing" was too small
  for his sex.
He was booked for exposure;
The judge said, on disclosure,
*"De minimis non curat lex."**

*The law does not concern itself with small things.

*"It's frightening . . . I don't know anyone anymore
who isn't a lawyer."*

CHAPTER SIXTEEN

THE COURTS

Old litigators never die— they just lose their appeal.

⚖

Litigators are proceduralists. They care less about who gets beheaded than about whether the guillotine is well oiled and running smoothly.

When a litigator receives a complaint charging his client with sawing the beaks off someone's prize pelicans, he doesn't say, "My God, Steve, that's disgusting. Is it true?"

Instead, he goes over the complaint with a fine-tooth comb, asking such questions as, "When was this complaint filed? Maybe the statute of limitations has run." Or, "Does the complaint say where the alleged sawing occurred? Maybe we could knock this out for filing in the wrong jurisdiction."

Obviously these questions have nothing to do with justice and fairness. But to the litigator they're an essential part of the system.

What system? The so-called "adversary system," which rests on the premise that out of the clash of lies, truth will emerge.

The basic problem with this system is that neither party has an interest in reaching a result that's fair for both sides. Each side goes for *all* the marbles— not just half. Each side obscures as much as possible.

The litigator's role in this system is to help his client obscure and obstruct. In *discovery*, for example, when each side gets to ask the other side for information, does either lawyer turn to his client and say, "Give him the papers, Fred; we have nothing to hide"?

"Would Your Honor please instruct the witness just to answer the question?"

Of course not. The lawyers procrastinate for months, ultimately either withholding the one relevant document, or providing it hidden in a train load of irrelevant garbage.

Both sides' lawyers then go back and forth to the judge, filing "Motions to Compel Disclosure." The process takes years —and generates gigantic legal fees.

The amazing thing is that litigators are unembarrassed by this role. They like it. When they describe themselves as "hired guns," they do so with *pride*.

To say the least, a litigator shouldn't be someone who embarrasses easily or thinks a lot about the end result of his life's labors. However, a lot of young lawyers get sucked into litigation because that's all law school has really taught them to do. Sadly, a number of perfectly nice people, fully capable of being embarrassed, end up as litigators.

LITIGATION POSTURING

Litigation is a form of low theater. Lawyers are constantly posturing, manifesting in their papers and in the courtroom passions that as lawyers they are incapable of feeling but that are calculated to enlist the support of the judge or jury.

Often the lawyers on opposing sides of a case do in fact hate each other, either because their fees hang in the balance, because they have convinced themselves that they genuinely feel the passions they pretend, or because they're inherently odious.

But usually their passions are totally contrived. Set forth below are seven of the most common litigation poses:

1. *Righteous indignation.* The lawyer's goal in adopting this pose is to suggest that his opponent's case is not only wrong on the law but also ethically questionable. Lawyers usually use this pose when there is no law on their side.

2. *Disdain.* This pose is commonly adopted by large firms defending wealthy corporations against one another. The idea is to convince the judge that the other firm has descended to the level of a two-bit ambulance chaser trying to squeeze a few bucks out of the first firm's successful but socially responsible client who in any event didn't *mean* to pour radioactive waste into the kindergarten's water supply.

3. *Intimacy.* This is the pose of well-known lawyers battling obscure solo practitioners. Hotshot lawyers use this pose, supplemented with bits of levity, to establish a personal relationship with the judge, suggesting without stating that *good* lawyers ("like you and me, Judge") can see that the opposing lawyer is a few tacos short of a platter.

4. *Persecution.* This pose is frequently utilized by civil rights lawyers representing minority defendants in cases brought by the federal government. It can be particularly advantageous where pre-trial questioning establishes that the jurors are totally illiterate and still admire Marion Barry.

5. *Bewilderment.* This is the pose of the lawyer whose opponents have just scored a direct hit, who have made a telling argument to which he has no reply. He resorts to this pose in a last-ditch effort to suggest that their argument makes no sense and is irrelevant to the facts of the case.

6. *Sincerity.* This "Would-I-lie-to-you?" pose is employed by defense lawyers attempting to counter popular (and reasonable) assumptions regarding the guilt of certain categories of clients—such as pro athletes charged with possession of cocaine or Congressmen brought up on morals charges.

7. *Disappointment.* With this pose a lawyer attempts to communicate that the devastating points just scored by his opponent are, to his sadness, underhanded and deceitful. Often the lawyer will season this pose with a touch of parental solicitude, as if for a child gone astray. This is the pose of a lawyer who sees his client about to go to jail—and his fee about to go out the window.

"Gerstein always enjoyed playing devil's advocate."

SPECIALTY COURTS

States have a variety of courts that dispense factory-line, bulk-process justice. You're bound to be dragged into one of these sooner or later, so it's good to know what they do.

Probate Court. This is where they resolve disputes over the property of dead people. If someone dies owning enough for round-trip cab fare to the Probate Court, people will fight over it.

Family Court. As every divorced person knows, you have to get permission to get divorced. Family court is where you go to request such permission—a degrading experience that will remind you of when you were in grade school and had to raise your hand to go to the bathroom.

Landlord–Tenant Court. This is where they decide whether a landlord *really* has to provide heat and hot water, and whether a tenant *really* has to pay his rent.

Juvenile Court. As Art Linkletter knew, kids do the darnedest things—like breaking windows, stealing cars, and sticking sharp objects into people they don't know. Juvenile court is where police take these high-spirited youngsters to decide if they should lose their allowances for a month or whether less severe discipline will suffice.

Small Claims Court. These courts decide disputes over sums up to, say, $2,000. Hence the nickname "small change" court.

*"Terrible day in court. I showed disdain when I meant
to show righteous indignation."*

YOU AND "THE COURT"

Ten Commandments of Courtroom Conduct

1. The judge is always "Your Honor" or "The Court."
2. The judge's clerk is always "Your Honor" or "The Court."
3. The judge is never "late," but often "the press of business" interrupts her schedule.
4. The judge's prior ruling is never "mistaken," but a contrary ruling may well be justified by "subsequent developments in the law."
5. The judge is always to be thanked for her thoughtful ruling, even if she has just insulted you personally and sentenced your client to life.
6. The judge has never "forgotten" anything, but frequently you must "refresh the Court's recollection" of key facts.
7. The judge has never "not gotten around to reading the papers," but frequently you must "draw the Court's attention" to key points therein.
8. The judge knows every relevant statute and case, so it is of course appropriate to introduce points of law with "As the Court knows . . ."
9. The judge will never "hold on" or "wait a second," but sometimes you may "beg the Court's pardon" or "pray for the Court's momentary indulgence."
10. The judge never has to "go to the bathroom," but often "the Court will take a brief recess."

CHAPTER SEVENTEEN

LEGAL ETHICS
(And Other Great Oxymorons)
⚖️

The very concept of legal ethics triggers guffaws within the general populace. It is viewed by most as a contradiction in terms, an oxymoron along the lines of "postal service," "military intelligence," "scholar-athlete," and "Justice Scalia."

The legal profession began purporting to care about legal ethics about a decade ago, but the old Code of Professional Responsibility was so general and obvious—e.g., "A Lawyer Should Represent a Client Competently" —that nobody took it seriously. Literally every question you might encounter in law school or on the bar exam could be answered with: "It's a tough issue, but I would never do it myself."

For extra points you could

Model Code of
Professional
Responsibility
and
Code of
Judicial
Conduct

American Bar Association

ABA
as amended February 1979

COURTESY AMONG LAWYERS: "AFTER YOU, DOGBREATH"

Time was, lawyers were extremely polite to one another. Courtroom conduct was the model of civility, and the refined intercourse of adversaries in litigation reflected Western civilization at its peak.

The worst thing one lawyer ever called another was "gravy-sucking pig," or perhaps "toejam."

The gentle and genteel (which is not to say gentile) days of the law appear to be behind us, however, as tempers go unchecked and mouths unmuzzled. Today's courtroom partakes more of the professional wrestling ring than the debating halls of Oxford.

A casual eavesdropper in the courtroom of the nineties is apt to hear references to "dubious assertions" and "theories of uncertain origin." A cursory perusal of briefs and deposition transcripts will likely turn up charges of "unfounded allegations" and "erroneous assumptions."

If this kind of language is commonplace, can slurs such as "questionable good faith" and "tendentious mischaracterization" be far behind?

Little wonder that ours is considered an X-rated profession.

---

add, "It's essential for a lawyer to avoid the appearance of impropriety, as well as the reality of it."*

Over the past five years, however, about half the states have adopted some version of the ABA-recommended Model Rules of Professional Conduct, which

are far more lawyerly—that is to say, lengthy and complex. Now law schools offer whole courses on the subject—with *grades*—and it's actually possible to *fail* the ethics portion of a bar exam!

These things being up to the individual states, the people at the ABA who drafted the model rules could afford to be high-minded and client-oriented; nobody was actually controlled by anything they came up with. The officials at the state level,

---

*Fact: I, Daniel R. White, solemnly swear that I wrote the foregoing statement no fewer than four times on the 1980 D.C. bar exam (the one I passed).

on the other hand, had to decide which rules would actually be adopted and *enforced*. The outcome, predictably, was a bit less noble.

The District of Columbia's struggle over Rule 3.2 is illustrative. The ABA's version of the rule requires, basically, that lawyers move litigation along as fast as possible and not slow things down just to avoid a final ruling or to jack up the costs for the other side. The actual language of the rule is that lawyers should "make reasonable efforts to expedite litigation consistent with the interests of the client."

But in the District of Columbia, where litigators control the bar (as they do most everywhere), they wanted something different. They wanted a rule

"Speed it up, Mr. Holman. They tried a case just like this on L.A. Law in less than an hour."

CLIENT SECRETS: THE ABA TAKES A COURAGEOUS STAND

Everybody knows how important it is for a lawyer to keep a client's secrets—so important, in fact, that the ABA's new Model Rules of Professional Conduct prohibit a lawyer from spilling the beans even if he knows a client is getting ready to commit serious financial harm or property damage.

The drafters of the Model Rules stood firm and courageous on one exception to this rule, however, allowing a lawyer to disclose client confidences if necessary to recover his fee.

In other words, lawyers will not—indeed, *may* not—disclose client confidences to avert something like a savings-and-loan disaster or arson in Yellowstone Park. But they can spill their guts if it will help them get paid.

Hey, principles are principles, but there's no need to let things get out of hand.

---

that would explicitly allow them to slow things down as much as possible. It should be up to the judge, they said, to keep things moving—even though, as every lawyer who doesn't have tofu for brains knows, a judge can rarely tell which motions have any real purpose to them.

The D.C. Court of Appeals, which has final say over the ethics rules there, ended up waffling and adopting *both* the ABA version (quoted above) and the D.C.-bar version, the latter being worded to prohibit delays that would serve "solely to harass or maliciously injure another"— which is basically no restric-tion at all, since how many motions are "solely" for anything?

The D.C. bar leaders weren't unhappy with the court's compromise, because they decided, on reflection (i.e., when somebody actually sat down and read the provisions at issue), that the ABA rule wasn't really so bad: Its mandate to expedite litigation "consistent with the interests of the client" could be interpreted to allow lawyers to screw around as much as they wanted. As the D.C. bar president put it in a recent article, with admirable candor (or appalling shamelessness—you be the judge), the rule in D.C. is now that "a lawyer may ethically pursue delay as a litigation tactic."

Maybe those ABA-drafters knew what they were doing after all.

HOW FAR CAN YOU GO?

How far *can* you go in fulfilling your ethical obligation to represent your client zealously? Suppose your client is charged with stabbing someone in a dark alley. Can you ethically contend—indeed, are you ethically *required* to contend—that he didn't actually stab the victim, but just happened to be holding the stiletto when the victim walked into it? . . . backwards? . . . twenty-three times?

Over the years, four tests have been developed for measuring which arguments are acceptable and which go too far:

1. *The Smell Test.* Also called the "cow pie test." The most stringent of the four standards, this one precludes you from making any argument that just doesn't smell right. Lots of arguments smell so bad that people in the courtroom will be checking the bottoms of their shoes.
2. *The Blush Test.* If you can make a given argument without turning visibly red, it passes. The stringency of this test, like that of the two tests below, varies depending on the shamelessness of the lawyer.
3. *The Gag Test.* Also called the "barf test." If you can utter a theory or alibi without upchucking from the outrageousness of your words, it passes. This test is usually reserved for rich clients in bad trouble.
4. *The Lightning Test.* Also called the "wrath of God test." This is an extremely liberal test, precluding only those arguments and theories so unsupportable that their very utterance is likely to cause lightning to strike you down as you speak. This test is usually reserved for *extremely* rich clients in *extremely* bad trouble.

CHAPTER EIGHTEEN

THE CREATIVE ART OF BILLING

Who Says There Are Only Twenty-Four Hours in a Day?

⚖

Anyone who says lawyers aren't creative and imaginative hasn't seen a lawyer fill out his time sheets.

If you hope to succeed in the law, it is essential to master the creative aspects of billing: As an associate, you can never tell partners how you really spent your time, and as a partner you can never tell clients what they're really being billed for.

Even if you're a lay person, it is important to understand the billing process. You'll still end up in hock to your lawyer, but at least you'll know where your money went.

The following two time sheets illustrate the legal mind at its creative best:

WHAT THE TIME SHEET *SAYS*

CLIENT: Danmark Goldberg, Inc.

ACTIVITY	TIME
Periodic review of active client litigation files	2 hours, 5 minutes
Phone conference with client personnel re same	1 hour
Subtotal:	3 hours, 5 minutes

CLIENT: PWCJR Oil Co.

Luncheon conference with client re outstanding matters, including lawsuit by employee labor union	2 hours, 20 minutes

CLIENT: Ryan Leg Development Spa

Reviewing, editing and revising modified loan documents	3 hours, 55 minutes

TOTAL TIME BILLABLE	9 hours, 20 minutes

WHAT THE TIME SHEET *SHOULD* SAY

CLIENT: Danmark Goldberg, Inc.
_____

ACTIVITY	TIME
Thinking about client's new receptionist during morning jog	30 minutes
Reading morning paper	25 minutes
Rummaging through client files for name and number of client's new receptionist	30 minutes
Getting coffee	15 minutes
Getting psyched to call client's new receptionist re dinner on Saturday night, including preparing notes to assist re same	1 hour, 15 minutes
Calling client's new receptionist re dinner on Saturday night	10 minutes
Subtotal:	3 hours, 5 minutes

CLIENT: PWCJR Oil Co.
_____

| |
--- | ---
Three-martini lunch with client at Chez St. Amand: |
•Discussing client's golf game and recent vacation in Barbados | 1 hour, 45 minutes
•Swapping ethnic jokes about employee union officials | 30 minutes
Subtotal: | 2 hours, 15 minutes

CLIENT: Ryan Leg Development Spa
_____

| |
--- | ---
Proofreading retyped loan documents | 1 hour, 20 minutes
Napping at desk | 20 minutes
Proofreading re-retyped loan documents | 1 hour, 10 minutes
Flirting with cute new associate | 25 minutes
Arranging for copying of re-re-re-typed loan documents | 40 minutes
Subtotal: | 3 hours, 55 minutes

TOTAL TIME BILLABLE | 9 hours, 20 minutes

"Airplanes and time zones are marvels of mankind. They've enabled me to bill 25 hours in a day."

MULTIPLE BILLING

Perhaps the most ingenious device known to the law was conceived in response to the popular misperception that there are only twenty-four hours in a day.

Double-billing, or billing two clients for the same increment of time, occurs most frequently on trips. A lawyer flying, say, from New York to Los Angeles to confer with two clients might bill the six hours of travel time to each. His rationale is that if he had made the trip for one client alone he'd have billed that client for all of the time—so why not bill all of it to each?

Some lawyers double bill as a matter of course. But none of them, not even the ones who triple and quadruple bill, acknowledge it publicly. They're greedy, not crazy. What they do is bury the double-billed time in the mountain of other items to be billed to the client in a month or two, and no one is the wiser.

The only way clients could monitor this practice would be to compare notes among themselves. They can't do that, of course; antitrust laws forbid it.

Antitrust laws arose about the same time as double billing.

CHAPTER NINETEEN

ATTORNEYS-AT-LOVE

Dealing with Romantic Feelings Toward a Lawyer

⚖️

You've heard the stories. Everyone has. They're not pretty. Maybe it's happened to someone you know. A friend or colleague. Maybe to someone you love—that's when it really hurts.

What on earth could possess someone to become romantically involved with a lawyer? To most people such an occurrence seems about as likely as falling in love with an old bowling shoe (an old *rented* bowling shoe).

A prominent sociologist has compared the phenomenon of lawyer-dating to the pet rock fad that swept the country some years ago—except, of course, for the tragic consequences. And the fact that playing with a pet rock offers the possibility of sexual gratification. Also, at a formal dinner party, you'll attract less attention with a pet rock. And a pet rock is more likely to pick up the tab for drinks. In fact, going out with a lawyer isn't much like playing with a pet rock at all.

Still, some people continue to do it—go out with lawyers, that is.

What is to be done? Sadly, for those already involved, precious little *can* be done. Anyone who has fallen in love with a lawyer is pretty far gone. The only real hope lies in prevention.

"I am, among other things, a Juris Doctor."

This can best be accomplished by having nothing to do with lawyers except when it's absolutely necessary, like when you're about to be hauled off to jail. Even then you might want to think about it. You know, taste the food, talk to your prospective cell mate—give it a chance.

For most people, avoiding lawyers comes as naturally as

breathing or, perhaps more appropriate, squashing a bug. You see a lawyer and think, there but for the grace of God goes my dog. You feel the same revulsion you feel for a drunk in the gutter—except the drunk might be pleasant company.

As difficult as it may be for most people to conceive of falling in love with a lawyer, a few seem to do it every year. What kind of perverse love are we talking about? It's difficult to describe, but if you've ever chatted with a sailor who's been away at sea for ten or twelve months, you have an idea of the sort of desperation involved.

It's similar to the unnatural craving that students at certain schools in New Hampshire experience toward the end of a long winter. It can lead to anything.

Consider the case of Marlene X. ("X" is not her real name.) We'll call her Marlene. She was an attractive young woman living in New York. She didn't get many dates, though. This is partly because she really wasn't all that attractive. (More than a few people who met her later commented, "I didn't know Ernest Borgnine was a transvestite.") She wasn't all that young, either. But she did live in New York.

Marlene was an unemployed former mortgage trader on Wall Street. The economic turmoil of the late eighties had cost many Wall Streeters their jobs.

WHAT TO BRING WITH YOU ON YOUR FIRST DATE WITH A LAWYER

If you're the reckless kind of person willing to date a lawyer, it's unlikely you'll be prudent enough to equip yourself for the occasion in advance. You will realize your mistake soon enough, however—ten minutes at the outside. At that point, if at all possible, pull over and grab the following items:

1. Yellow legal pad
2. No-Doz—industrial strength
3. Body condom
4. Lomotil
5. English-Latin/Latin-English dictionary
6. Sony Walk-Man
7. Cash

SPOTTING LAWYERS OUT ON THE TOWN

In a better world, lawyers would never set foot out of their offices. They'd just live there—eating, sleeping, billing. Some New York firms have already attained this plateau.

Many lawyers still wander the streets, however, and running into one can ruin an otherwise perfectly enjoyable Saturday night.

You're a friendly person. You enjoy meeting new people. But you have to draw the line somewhere. Hey, if you wanted to be bored, you'd be back at work talking to your accountant.

Suppose you spot a lawyer near you in a bar or restaurant. What do you do? First, look around for others; they hang out in packs.

Then, if it's a guy, try spilling a drink on his trousers; the prospect of losing the crease will send him packing. If it's a woman, aim for the legs; she'll have backup pantyhose in her purse, but the thought of being down to her last pair will have her out the door.

If a lawyer should take the clearly inappropriate step of initiating conversation with you, call the authorities and have him physically ejected from the premises. Don't worry about hurting his feelings; he's used to this type of treatment. Some lawyers go out in public *wanting* abuse, craving that moment of self-definition when they hit the sidewalk or the grill of a passing truck.

What if you're not sure the person in question is a lawyer? When you're eleven bourbons into the evening, you may not be able to tell one from a foreigner who's just off the boat and hasn't mastered standard English.

And it's not as if you can just come out and ask, because what if he's *not* a lawyer? Then you've probably got a fight on your hands.

Besides, what are the chances of anybody admitting to that kind of thing, especially when he's out in public trying to "pass"?

Check the person out with one of the following tests:

1. Mention that you recently had your appendix removed,

and you could swear you feel the outline of surgical clamps still in your abdomen. Then stare into his face. If his pupils dilate and saliva appears, have him thrown out.

2. Assert that the legal profession should be regulated by a panel of lay people. If this triggers a strident attack on politicians, doctors, and custom tailors, have him thrown out.

3. Tell him he has the look of a paralegal or legal secretary. If this causes him to flinch, redden, and sputter (not to be confused with a Denver law firm by that name), have him thrown out.

4. State that you favor no-fault insurance legislation. If he embarks on an outraged polemic on the God-given right of every American to sue anybody for anything, have him thrown out.

5. Declare that you've long considered briefcases and dictaphones to be emblematic of a truly advanced society. If he nods in agreement, have him thrown out.

6. Mention that your highest admiration goes to the geniuses of the world who can understand the U.S. tax code. If he smiles, puffs out his chest, and launches into a discussion of offshore tax shelters and generation-skipping transfers, have him thrown out. (You may also catch an accountant or two with this trick—no loss.)

If, despite your best efforts, a lawyer causes irreparable harm to your night on the town, don't just get depressed, chalking it off as another scoreless inning in the game of life. Get even!

First, accept his lousy business card. Accept two or three. You never know when you'll back into somebody's car in a parking lot and need to leave some form of I.D.

Second, tell him you were just this minute—the darnedest coincidence!—talking to someone who's looking to hire a lawyer. And then give him the name of that insurance salesman who's been bugging you for years.

Marlene had been laid off a bit before the turmoil began, but that's another story. At the moment she had lots of time on her hands, which she used not only to eat until she resembled a zeppelin, but also to hit every resort in the Western Hemisphere in hopes of meeting Mr. Right.

Enter Andrew K. Filbert—his real name; so what if a lawyer is publicly humiliated? He was a conscientious if modestly talented associate at a large corporate firm in Manhattan, and equipped with about the same social appeal as Marlene.

Andrew and Marlene met at a Club Med south of the border. They were both fighting for space at the hors d'oeuvre table, hurling food of every sort in the general direction of their heads.

Perhaps by fate they simultaneously made a grab for the same hors d'oeuvre, the last one of those miniature hot dogs you eat with toothpicks—and their hands touched. Although both were initially repulsed, their long-starved sexual appetites quickly took over, and they left hand in hand—which repulsed everyone else, but Marlene and Andrew were way beyond caring about that.

Their immediate infatuation yielded to passion. They spent every night together for the next month. So inflamed was Marlene's ardor that she could overlook Andrew's insistence on wearing his three-piece suits to bed. "I think it's the vest," Andrew would say. "It makes me feel so masterful."

By the end of the month they were engaged.

Marlene's enchantment soon turned to frustration. As time went on, Andrew began dragging himself home later and later. It reached the point that Marlene wouldn't know if he was coming home at all, and when he did, usually around midnight, he would go straight to sleep (still wearing his suit, as mentioned).

For a while Marlene suspected Andrew of seeing another woman. Some of his sleep-talking sounded vaguely licentious—terms like "joinder of parties," "ejectment," and "post-trial briefs." As blind as love is, however, Marlene was able to make a realistic assessment of the chances of another woman becoming interested in Andrew, and she put that thought out of her mind.

Abstinence wasn't the worst of Marlene's problems with Andrew. They didn't seem to communicate anymore. Andrew had taken to addressing Marlene in rude, condescending tones, which she knew he had picked up from the way senior partners at the firm addressed Andrew, and the way everyone at the firm addressed non-paying clients. Rather than simply talking with her, Andrew seemed to be lecturing her, and he had the strange habit of summarizing his argument at the outset and reserving three minutes for rebuttal.

Marlene considered breaking off the engagement. Everyone said her goldfish was better company, even though it had been floating at the top of the tank for a month. But it's a hard world for short, pudgy, odd-looking, untalented former mortgage traders, and she decided to go through with it.

Only after she had had her first child and realized how much it would be like Andrew—try to imagine a hairless possum in pinstripes—did Marlene appreciate the full measure of her mistake.

Marlene's story is a sad one, the story of a wasted life. But it need not be your story as well.

Let us all learn the lesson of her misfortune: The only way to handle romantic feelings toward a lawyer is not to have any.

Can you find the lawyer in this picture?

CHAPTER TWENTY

YOU AND YOUR LAWYER

Finding Him, Using Him, Keeping Him in His Place

⚖

Sooner or later it happens to everybody. Your life is going along just fine, the car is almost paid for, you just got a big promotion, your sex life is finally heating up—and suddenly disaster strikes. Your playful Great Dane—good old Gaylord—dismembers a small child; you have a few drinks and on the way home decide to run that yellow light, only to notice too late the local sheriff's elderly mother stepping into the crosswalk; your wife finds some pink lace underwear in your glove compartment and doesn't buy your story about how much more comfortable you find them than your regular shorts during the summer heat.

Law books are full of such tales of disaster. What makes them disasters is that when they happen, you have to get a lawyer —Your Lawyer.

You've hoped against hope that you'd never have to do it. You've never felt comfortable around lawyers. You've never associated them with the good things in life.

But now there's no choice. Like appendicitis, your legal problem won't just go away. You have to *do* something about it— and you can't do it on your own.

The analogy to appendicitis is instructive: Getting rid of your legal problem, like having an organ removed, is painful, costly

"I find it helps to remember that the client is the one in trouble. Nobody's talking about sending me to jail."

(your Lawyer will do a wallet-ectomy on you), and will leave you slightly scarred.

But since it has to be done, you want it done right. This requires careful attention to certain points.

Selecting Your Lawyer

How do you go about the critical task of selecting Your Law-

yer? Just let your fingers do the walking? Answer a television ad for one of those low-priced, polyester-vested hucksters who share walkup offices with the Acme Finance Company?

In law, as in life, you get what you pay for. You should choose Your Lawyer the same way you would a doctor—and you don't look for bargain-basement prices when it comes to the person who's going to remove your adenoids, do you?

DOCTORS V. LAWYERS

"Doc, I have this debenture that's been acting up again."

Doctors and lawyers are notoriously unfriendly to one another. This seems strange at first, because they attended the same schools, they live in the same neighborhoods—they're natural allies against . . . the poor.

Nevertheless they're hostile. In part this is because lawyers are intimidated by doctors. Lawyers are in awe of anybody who can get an ambulance to come *to him*. More important, however, is old-fashioned envy on the part of lawyers—envy involving more than just the obvious things, like the fact that doctors get to see people naked whenever they want.

Lawyers also envy the superior status and prestige enjoyed by the medical profession, the evidence of which is everywhere. Doctors get special license plates, for example, which permit them to park in places normally reserved for people with no legs.

Doctors get to be called "Doctor," whereas nobody calls even the best lawyers "Esquire." Sure, lawyers get to put "Attorney-at-Law" on their embossed letterhead, but this is just a curiosity; have you ever heard of an attorney-at-anything else? Attorney-at-Plumbing? Attorney-at-Painting-Lines-on-Highways?

Someone who graduates at the bottom of his medical school class still gets to be called "Doctor," whereas someone who graduates at the bottom of his law school class is called "Waiter!"*

Today the very word "doctor" is synonymous with "skill" and "finesse," whereas "lawyer" is more often associated with "deviousness" and "cunning." Think about it: Have you ever heard of any professional basketball players called "Lawyer J"?

Along the same lines, have you ever known anyone to stand up in a theater and cry, "Is there a lawyer in the house?"

Finally, it's common knowledge that while medical schools remain somewhat competitive, everybody in the country could get into *some* law school. Just think about the lawyers you know: Some are bright enough, but how many will ever be picking up any prizes in Stockholm?

*Or "Your Honor!"

GET A REFERRAL

A referral is your best bet. Ask your family, friends, or minister. Do *not* ask your doctor. Doctors detest lawyers more than cancer, heart disease, or socialized medicine. The mere idea that you're on the verge of hiring and giving money to a lawyer might induce your doctor subconsciously to leave scissors, clamps, even a Phillips-head screwdriver in your abdomen. (This is particularly troublesome if you're just in for a throat culture.)

The problem with the referral approach to finding a lawyer is that no one ever has anything good to say about a lawyer. Even your minister is likely to describe the lawyers he knows in language more commonly heard from dock workers. Still, if you can get a few names, you're on your way.

DO COMPARATIVE SHOPPING

Set up appointments with five or six lawyers—as many as you can stomach. Remember that although the one you eventually hire will bill you for the precious time you squander in this first interview, the several you *don't* hire will have to absorb the loss. (If one of them tries to hit you up for a couple

of hundred dollars, feel free to use the bill for kitty litter—it'll never be worth his while to sue you.)

Your Appointment

("Just the facts, Ma'am.")

Okay. So you've set up your first appointment with a lawyer. Relax. If he turns out to be even worse than you feared, you still have hundreds more to chose from, without even leaving your immediate neighborhood. Console yourself with the thought that no matter how bad things are, at least *you're* not a lawyer.

As the appointment day draws near, collect your thoughts. Figure out what it is you want Your Lawyer to do for you. You're going to pay through the nose for it; you might as well get your money's worth.

When you arrive at Your Lawyer's building, go straight to the office directory on the wall of the lobby and note four things:
1. how many lawyers there are in Your Lawyer's firm;
2. how many floors in the building are occupied by Your Lawyer's firm;
3. how many floors there are between the floor on which Your Lawyer is located and the highest floor occupied by the firm; and

4. how close the firm is to the top of the building.

These trifling facts, although of no consequence whatsoever to most people, are highly important to Your Lawyer. In dealing with this person, it is important that you understand the thoughts that dominate all his waking hours, even as those hours are being billed to you.

Next go up to Your Lawyer's floor, and ask the receptionist to let him know you are there. Do not be put off by having to wait longer than you do when renewing your license plates. Be happy that at least you do not have to stand in line.

In the waiting area, savor the luxury of filthy but thoughtfully spent lucre: the Persian rugs, the exotic plants, the Renaissance masterpieces adorning the walls. Try not to think about who's paying for them.

STAY COOL

Eventually a secretary will arrive to escort you to the inner sanctum, where you will finally cast eyes upon the curiosity who may become Your Lawyer. Keep your wits about you now. Take note of various points of manner, such as whether he steps forward to greet you openly, or conducts the interview from behind his desk (so that you cannot be sure he is wearing trousers); whether he asks his secretary to hold all calls, or subjects you to interruptions from his other clients' parole officers.

Above all, do not be intimidated. Ask him where he went to law school and how high he graduated in his class. Make him explain the difference between herringbone and tweed.

Remember: He's not Your Lawyer yet.

DISCUSS THE FEE

An essential matter for you to raise on this first visit is the fee. Lawyers never bring it up on their own. They can be strangely cryptic in this regard, purporting to disdain the subject as too crass for discussion.

Do not be taken in by this pose. Here, as in other areas, lawyers resemble ladies of the night: The most charming can be the most vicious when it comes to collecting their fees. Recall that fee-collection time is one of the rare occasions when a lawyer becomes free to violate the much touted sanctity of the attorney–client privilege.

Reject evasive answers. You don't want to discover too late that Your Lawyer's casual reference to "my standard rate" means $400 per hour. Neither should you rest easy with the assurance, "Oh, I think we can work out something that will be mutually satisfactory." Hey, if you weren't desperate, you wouldn't be paying him *anything*.

Be prepared to have to work for an answer. He might attempt full-scale diversionary tactics:

That's a good question, Ms. Benkendorff, and I'm glad you had the presence of mind to raise it at the outset. Too often, I think, lawyers are so busy striving to advance their clients' interests that they lose sight of these kinds of questions and neglect to establish any true understanding—or what could be called a meeting of the minds—as to how it will all shake out in the long run. Why, I recall one case out in California . . .

When this romp through irrelevance terminates, repeat the question. Do so again and again until either you get an answer or the cleaning people come in to vacuum and turn off the lights.

You Call the Shots

The basic rule here is: Your Lawyer works for you, not vice versa. You pay the bills, you call the shots.

Early on in the relationship you will find Your Lawyer telling you what you can or cannot do, or what you must or

mustn't do. Nip this in the bud. Tell him what *you* want, and if he can't make it happen, let him know you're prepared to take your business down the road. You will be surprised at how quickly he will determine, after a little additional research, that what you want seems to be possible after all.

MONITOR YOUR LAWYER'S WORK

Monitor closely the work on your case, contract, or whatever. Ask for periodic, detailed statements of account. If Your Lawyer gets the idea that you aren't too worried about the size of the bill, it will expand in ways you couldn't imagine. It will manage to take on expensive dinners, exotic travel, and fertilizer for his lawn, not to mention peripheral research that would have been done anyway for other clients—things that AT&T may not mind subsidizing, but you do.

Don't go overboard with this monitoring. Even a twenty-second phone conversation with Your Lawyer can cost as much as dinner for eleven at an expensive restaurant—that's *with* wine.

The fact is that anything Your Lawyer does for you starts the meter running. It doesn't matter if he's just *thinking* about sending you a copy of a brief or a recent statement of expenses. If he's doing anything that so much as reminds him of you, you'll be billed for the time.

Keeping Your Lawyer in Perspective

It's important to remember that Your Lawyer is, after all, only a lawyer—not a psychotherapist, minister, or even a friend. That you come to him in trouble, and that you tell him intimate things that not even your doctor or milkman knows about, does not alter the basic fact that his interest in you is commercial.

Your Lawyer may sound personally interested in the details of your gall-bladder operation. You may appreciate his expressions of outrage as you describe your wife's infidelities, or your husband's violent tendencies as he reaches his sixth martini every evening. But remember that with each word you utter, Your Lawyer's meter is clicking away.

If that meter isn't running, Your Lawyer isn't listening.

CHAPTER TWENTY-ONE

LEGAL GLOSSARY

Of Foreign—and Forked— Tongues

⚖

Accord and Satisfaction—1. Resolution of a claim for breach of contract, whereby the parties agree to alter the original terms. 2. Carnal indulgence in the backseat of a Japanese car.

Action—Lawsuit. A term used by lawyers to distract the client from the fact that nothing is happening in his case.

Adultery—The crime of having more fun than society considers it seemly for an adult to have.

Affidavit—A client's sworn statement of whatever facts his lawyer believes necessary to win the case.

Affirmative Action—As originally conceived, the preferential hiring of minorities and women. These days, hiring *anyone.*

A Fortiori—Latin, "For a still stronger reason." A term used by lawyers to link an indisputable premise to an inexplicable conclusion.

Allegation—A supposedly factual statement pertaining to a lawsuit. *See* allegory, fable.

AMA—American Medical Association. An investment club specializing in underwater real estate.

Ambulance Chasing—What personal-injury lawyers refer to as "client development."

Amicus Curiae—Latin, "Friend of the curious." The person who works at the information desk in federal courthouses.

Arbitrator—An independent negotiator. Derived from a combination of *arbitrary* and *traitor*.

Arguendo—Latin, "For the sake of argument," or hypothetically speaking. Not to be confused with "Innuendo," a popular Italian suppository.

Bankruptcy—Life after debt.

Bigamy—Double jeopardy.

Brief—A legal term which, to the extent that it suggests brevity, constitutes the only monosyllabic oxymoron in the English language.

Briefcase—A leather lunch pail.

Capital Gains Tax—Accrual and unusual punishment.

Controlled Substance—Any of various recreational drugs seized from traffickers for use by off-duty police officers.

Deadwood—Anyone in your firm senior to you.

Delaware—A fictional locality maintained in perpetuity by the U.S. Postal Service as a forwarding address for large corporations.

Dictaphone—A battery-powered device beloved by lawyers for its inability to fall asleep during legal monologues.

Euthanasia—A system of early retirement often urged on highly paid senior lawyers by their younger partners.

Fee Tail—A restricted form of real estate ownership. Not to be confused with "free tail" (*see* Club Med).

Force Majeure—An irresistible force that keeps you from performing your contractual obligations—such as a hurricane, flood, war, or the discovery that you could make a greater profit elsewhere.

Habeas Corpus—Latin, "You've got a body." A pickup line at bar conventions.

Hung Jury—A divided jury. Ironic term, because if the jury is hung, the defendant isn't. (*Compare well*-hung jury.)

J.D.—Latin, *Juris Doctor*. A *doctoral* degree given to *bachelor*-level students who have yet to *master* any practical skills.

Judge—A unicameral legislative body.

Learned Hand—A prominent federal judge, named after a legendary sixteenth-century Turkish eunuch. No relation to Learned Tongue.

Chief Judge Learned Hand,
U.S. Court of Appeals

Litigation—A basic right in the American legal system, which guarantees every aggrieved person his decade in court.

Legal Pad—1. The residence of a hip lawyer. 2. That extra something built into a lawyer's bill.

Melvin Belli—1. (In)famous U.S. trial lawyer. 2. Latin, "Meet me in Bhopal."

Mother-in-Law—As distinguished from a mother-in-equity, someone who has no discretion.

Nuisance—Wrongful interference with someone's use and enjoyment of his property—for example, your thoughtless upstairs neighbor who insists on playing loud rock music at times when decent people like you are trying to sleep—not to mention the ill-bred insomniac downstairs who has taken to banging on his ceiling with a broomstick just because he can't appreciate the tasteful melodies (and other rhythmic sounds) that emanate from your apartment at various reasonable times.

Objection—The cry of a lawyer who sees truth about to sneak into the courtroom.

Obscenity—Prurient books, films, and other materials. Difficult to identify, except for U.S. Justice Potter "I know it when I see it, dadgumit!" Stewart.

Oyez—A cry of pain traditionally issued three times in anticipation of exceptionally boring legal proceedings. Derived from Yiddish, "Oy vay! Oy vay! Oy vay!"

Parachuter—Someone who enters a law firm laterally, i.e., after working at another firm. Useful for reminding junior lawyers that they're replaceable.

Paralegal—A legal secretary who can't type.

Parole—A conditional release from prison, usually for the

purpose of allowing the convict to demonstrate the inadequacy of the original sentence.

Per Curiam—Latin, "Nobody here will take the blame."

Physician—1. The ideal plaintiff. 2. The ideal defendant. (*Compare* Fort Knox.)

Pro bono publico—Latin, "For the public good." Refers to legal services performed for ingrates.

Res Ipsa Loquitur—Latin, "It won't stop talking." A legal defense to the crime of killing parrots and myna birds.

Statutory Rape—The crime of sexual relations with someone whom the law deems too young to give meaningful consent. *Compare* Statutory French Kissing.

Tax Lawyer—Someone with a flair for numbers but without the personality to be an accountant.

Stare Decisis—Latin, "To stare decisively." The process by which a witness to a crime indicates which of the subjects in a lineup was the perpetrator.

Vagina—Aren't you a little old to be looking up words like this?

Watered Stock—1. Overpriced securities. 2. Bloated cattle.

Will—A device that lets you wait until you're out of harm's way before revealing how you really felt about your spouse and children.

Once you've finished *Still the Official Lawyer's Handbook*, you're better prepared for a legal career than any sad product of Yale or Columbia. Unlike the graduates of conventional legal institutions—indebted to the hilt and helpless prey to experienced vultures—you're ready for clients!

Don't be modest about the insights you've acquired. Tear out the diploma on the following page, frame it, and display it prominently in your office.

You've earned it.

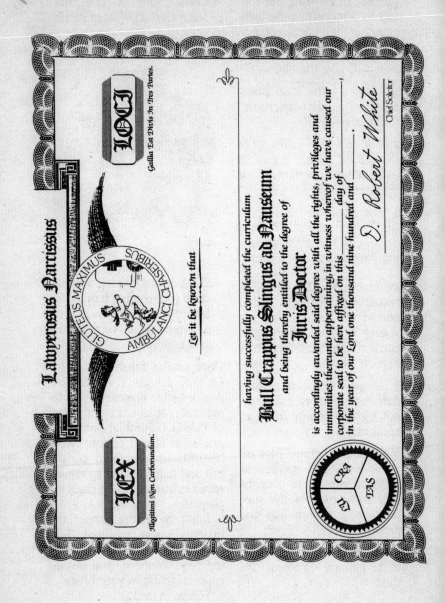

Lawyerosus Narcissus

GLUTEUS MAXIMUS AMBULANCI CHASERIBUS

LOCI
Gallia Est Divis In Tres Partes.

LEX
Illegitimi Non Carborundum.

having successfully completed the curriculum

Bull Crappus Slingus ad Nauseum

and being thereby entitled to the degree of

Juris Doctor

Let it be known that

is accordingly awarded said degree with all the rights, privileges and immunities thereunto appertaining; in witness whereof we have caused our corporate seal to be here affixed on this _____ day of _____ in the year of our Lord one thousand nine hundred and _____,

D. Robert White
Chief Solicitor

VERITAS